YOU

FINANCIAL GPS

THE EASIER PATH TO A WEALTHY LIFE

BEN CHAPMAN

Self-Published by Ben Chapman

First published in Great Britain in 2023

ISBN 978-1-7394910-0-0

Produced by Softwood Self-Publishing

Printed in Great Britain by TJ Books

This book is dedicated to my late mum Veronica Chapman, who sadly passed away in 2019. She was a truly inspirational person. If I told her I was thinking about writing this book, I know exactly what she would have said: "What are you waiting for? Go for it!"

She looked at the world as a place full of opportunity and experiences waiting to be explored. She understood that life is worth living. She gave me an enthusiasm for life and a sense of optimism that has stayed with me to this day.

My hope is that this book can instil in you the same outlook and help you focus on and make the most of the opportunities that lie ahead. I would like to thank all my friends, family and colleagues for sharing important feedback on the upcoming chapters, but I'd especially like to thank every client who has helped me as much as I have them by sharing their life goals, aspirations and experiences with me and trusting me to advise them to improve their lives and finances. Their perspectives have helped me shape the content of this book.

Contents

Introduction

I have set out to write a short book that will make your life easier.

You may have bought this book because you have made a conscious choice to invest in yourself and improve your life. Or perhaps some kind friend or family member has given you the book as a gift with the recommendation that it is worth reading. If this is the case, I am delighted, as this is the intention I set out with. It also means that it really is worth reading!

It is important to say at this point that this is not in any way financial advice. Financial advice is, quite rightly, highly regulated. I cannot know your personal circumstances and so I cannot offer 'advice' – but I can offer a great deal of useful information and I can tell you what other people tend to do and what behaviours, in general, are successful or unsuccessful. The book is a guide and refers to high level concepts. If it encourages you to make any changes to your finances, I strongly encourage you to seek professional advice.

Investing in yourself really is the single best venture you can embark on and, in my opinion, the best dividend payer in the market and the essence of compounding returns. I'm a huge advocate of having a growth mentality and seeking ways to be better at things. Educating yourself and practicing this mindset ensures that in the future you will fail less and succeed more. And when you do fail – because everyone fails sometimes when they try something new – you can be happy that it was simply the price of a lesson that takes you one step closer to success.

If you read this book, I know for a fact that you will know more than you do now, understand your friends and family better and have a better life than if you hadn't read it. How do I know that? Because I'm going to provide you with a roadmap to make your life better.

So, on that note, congratulations! Your life has just got better.

People ask me all the time, "Ben, what do you do?"

The simplest and best answer I've found is that I make people's lives easier. That's a bold claim, but I know it's true.

I had to come up with an elevator pitch for the services I offer a few years ago as part of a networking event I attended. This is when I first came up with the idea of the Financial GPS. We all use GPS to help us get around. You simply tell your device where you want to go, and it plots a course and tells you how to get there. It tells you how long it's going to take, gives you a selection of transport methods or different routes if you are driving and then guides you along the way. If you get stuck in a traffic jam, take a wrong turn on the street or maybe get off at the wrong tube station, it's right there to give you the next best route and keep you on track. You can take the road with tolls or the scenic route, and you can plan stop offs along the way, but it never takes its eye off getting you to your destination.

This is exactly what I do for people. It's perhaps unfortunate there isn't a computer system or app that could provide our financial GPS, but it would take a very clever programmer to take into account the different psychology of individuals and how their perspectives change through the course of their lives. People don't always behave logically; humans are primarily emotional beings. And the constantly shifting pattern of world events that affects our finances can't be programmed into any app; there are simply too many moving pieces.

The human element is vital. Over the last 20-odd years of working with clients, I have learned to listen for the 'why' in every human story.

Listening isn't easy. It's a skill you have to practice. We naturally want to jump in with our own story or furnish a question with our own answer, when it is essential that the other person comes to their own conclusion and supplies their own answer. Understanding the 'why' is paramount. I have read probably 50+ books on human psychology, philosophy, influencing people, self-development, management theories and body language, in addition to all the technical books and journals about finance. I've taken every examination that I can in my profession and am a Chartered Financial Planner and a Fellow of the Chartered Insurance institute. I won two separate prizes for the highest exam marks in the country when I completed my Diploma and Discretionary Fund Management exams. I love to study; I enjoy taking exams and improving my knowledge.

All of my reading and the questions I ask people have been in the pursuit of understanding why we do what we do. Once we know this, then the 'how' and the 'what' become so much clearer. It's like driving through fog and then suddenly it begins to clear. The road ahead is plain to see; driving becomes automatic and, most importantly, enjoyable. You stop squinting, straining to see the path ahead and stressing about wrong turns, because you can see the way ahead clearly again. You begin to look forward to experiencing the things that lie in front of you.

I'm a curious person by nature and I have been fortunate to have conducted thousands of interviews with people about their lives. I've sat down with people from all walks of life – the rich and the poor, the lucky and the unlucky, the old and the young – and have been lucky enough to hear the story of their lives. I enjoy hearing the intentions and dreams of younger people setting off in life and the wisdom of hindsight that older generations have bestowed on me. I have seen clients go through entire lifecycles and experienced the highest of highs and the lowest of lows with them.

What never ceases to amaze me when I sit down with a new client and ask them what they are saving for, what they are going to buy with their money, what they aspire to, what would make their lives better, and what they worry about, is that the answers are always unique to that person but also familiar. We all generally want variants of the same things, and for the same reasons. We're all human after all. We just perceive and communicate things differently.

Money and wealth are a means for us to live our lives; a resource to facilitate the actions we take and enable the lifestyles we want. A lack of or an excess of wealth or money will often lead to harder choices. You can live a wealthy life as a rich or poor person and, equally, live a life of destitution as a rich or poor person. The purpose of this book is to explore the major catalysts and events in life and help you to look at your 'why' in each situation, exploring the potential paths forward at each of the crossroads.

I'm going to offer you this experience about major life events so that you can get to your personal destination faster and more easily. I will share with you what successful people do and what the less successful tend to do – but, more importantly, why they do it. You may reflect on this and see yourself in some of the examples. I hope this reaffirms some of your decision-making processes but also improves many more future decisions.

I will make generalisations throughout the book and try to simplify concepts and situations so that any decisions remain high level and are easier to make. This will hopefully provide you with a mid-line to base things on but, obviously, your own situation is unique to you. When I use the phrase 'most people' and 'we' and you feel the subsequent statement doesn't apply to you, consider how many of your friends or family this might apply to. Remember this might not be you now but there is a good chance your future self may feel this way, or you will look back and remember your old self used to think a certain way. It's always good to self-reflect and appreciate the evolution of your character.

We constantly evolve throughout our lives and improve our approach to life by using trial and error to work out what we like and what we don't; what works for us and what doesn't. If we do X, then this will always lead to Y. However, this is only true for certain periods of time. The decisions we make, and the reasons why, may have been perfect in our twenties, but fast forward to age 60 and this is not likely to be the case. We are highly likely to make different decisions because we have become different people. We are always evolving, as is the world. The outcomes we want become different as we age so we need to learn new habits and appreciate the factors that affect our decision making.

There are short, medium and long-term goals and destinations for all of us. The most important thing to remember is that you will eventually reach these destinations and will need to make decisions along the way. The better decisions you make now, the more successful destinations you will arrive at and the easier new decisions will be to make when you get there.

We like maps, routes, guides, tips and shortcuts. The path already travelled is one that is always appealing, yet we crave the exploration and excitement of our own journey. Reading this book will give you a map to refer to on your own journey. It will help you to make your life simpler and easier. I've never met anyone who wanted things to be more complicated or more difficult.

The goal is to achieve the best range of possible outcomes. Nobody can guarantee any outcome and for every decision there are a range of possibilities and possible futures. It's the same destination for all of us, but we will all have very different journeys.

There is no better time to make decisions than now. One of my favourite sayings is: "The best time to plant a tree was 20 years ago. The second-best time is now." If you want success and growth in the future, the best time to act is now.

Part 1
Life Stages

This opening section reviews some of the key financial aspects of our lives from decade to decade, reflecting on what most of us need and choose to spend our money on as we progress through the various stages of life, and on some of the most important decisions we can make in order to ensure a healthy financial future.

We are all living longer. A healthy young person today has a very good chance of living to a ripe old age – certainly to the age of 90 or beyond. It is important to plan for that likely outcome, financially speaking, so that we can enjoy every stage of our increasingly long lives to the full.

Our first decade

For many of us, our earliest memories start with the most momentous event of our lives at that time: starting playgroup or nursery or some equivalent form of early schooling. A study published in 2021, based on over 20 years of research, suggested that most people have memories that start when they are young as two and a half years old.[1]

For those of us who are lucky enough to be born into a happy and supportive family environment, our earliest years are years of indulgence. Our parents do whatever they can to make us

[1] Full article: What is your earliest memory? It depends (tandfonline.com)

happy. All of us go through the usual childhood illnesses, but in general these episodes don't stay in our memories. A more significant illness after our first few years of life does tend to leave an imprint, and a truly serious childhood illness is likely to be life-defining, as are neglect or abuse. The majority of us are lucky enough to have little more to worry about than colds, sore throats, chickenpox and the like, all of which are quickly forgotten.

Encountering the outside world, in the form of our earliest schooling and social interactions, can be hugely significant. Humans are social animals, and we are sensitive to our social environment from a very young age. Young children begin to get their first inkling as to where they stand in the social world. They may enter a world of ease and privilege, or they may begin to encounter worrying signs of prejudice and hostility.

Working as a financial advisor, I am often struck by the effect that our early upbringing has on our attitude to money. People who have grown up in an environment where money is scarce, tend to have a different attitude than people who have had more comfortable upbringings. The extremes – real poverty or significant wealth – leave deeper marks. I have even noticed that what might be called the 'political' environment people grow up in can affect their attitude to money. People who grow up in left-leaning family environments can be uneasy in later life about tax planning, for example, because they instinctively associate the concept with 'tax avoidance'. Our attitudes to wealth generation can also be formed in these formative years: the children of entrepreneurs are likely to have a different approach to the concept of owning businesses, employing other people and generating wealth than the children of parents who have spent their lives being employed by organisations of one sort or another.

Our earliest years are also when our moral sense begins to develop, as we begin to learn what is acceptable and unacceptable; what is 'good' and what is 'bad'. This can shape our attitude to what are known as Environmental, Social and Governance (ESG) investments. Some people are uncomfortable investing in what they see as unfettered capitalism, 'red in tooth and claw', and they look for investments that can be seen to be more socially acceptable. Others are comfortable investing in whatever businesses offer the best returns on their money.

Our earliest responses to having money for the first time can also be very influential. Presents received at birthdays and holidays are hugely exciting, but there is something very different about receiving cash. Perhaps relatives give us money when they visit the family. Maybe the tooth fairy is generous when we start to lose our milk teeth. Perhaps we are rewarded with pocket money by our parents for carrying out various household chores, or we have a paper round or some other way of earning small amounts of money, giving us a first understanding that effort can be rewarded and that those rewards can build up into a useful resource.

Wherever our money came from, we quickly get a sense of what it can buy in the immediate term, and we may begin to think about putting that money aside so that we can make a more significant purchase later. Many parents open tax-free savings accounts for children, such as Junior Individual Savings Accounts (JISAs) to encourage new saving habits, and the children begin to see their money increasing in value. One important thing to note is that every JISA officially becomes an ISA and the property of the individual when they turn 18. This provides a significant moment of choice for any teenager: to blow the cash or invest it in their future. Those who have had some coaching and guidance from parents early on are more likely to have this earmarked for a first car, a period of travel, further education or even a deposit for a home, and they spend it carefully. Those without coaching may tend to dip into the money for more frivolous adventures but rarely do I see cases of the funds being spent carelessly. By 18 most people have a good sense of the value of money and an appreciation this was saved for something better.

Even though our first decade of life is a period of financial innocence in which we are not required to take any meaningful actions or make any important decisions, it is interesting and perhaps surprising how much our early experience can shape our attitudes to money in later life.

From 10 to 20

This is a decade dominated for most of us by education, and of course by the dramatic change from childhood to early adulthood. Things get highly emotional and most of us begin to challenge the status quo. We get a bit rebellious.

The education that we receive can be hugely influential. In the UK, a key differential is whether we get a state education or a private education. Some state schools are undeniably substandard; many are genuinely excellent. A good state education has the benefit of introducing young people to potential new friends from very different backgrounds, including the children of many quite wealthy parents who simply choose not to send their kids to private schools. This has great benefits in preparing young people for work experience in our muti-cultural, meritocratic society. However, the increasing spread of wealth through all sectors of British society has meant that children attending private schools are also from increasingly diverse backgrounds.

The key differentiator between state and private schools in

the UK, in my opinion, is that private schools are very driven to discover what children's real strengths are. They are paid, in effect, by result, and parents who send their children to private schools (and the children themselves) are more aware of market forces. Their parents are very conscious that they are paying substantial amounts of money for a private education, and they expect value for money. The schools are equally conscious of this central fact, and they work hard to deliver value for money: they are very motivated to find exactly what it is that children really excel at so they can encourage this, and their students will be demonstrably successful, because they have been encouraged to discover the things they have a real affinity for and are good at. Private schools have the resources to allow children to explore a range of activities that may not be readily available at state schools: a wider range of academic subjects to choose from; the chance to try out less mainstream sports; a wider range of musical and dramatic activities to explore; more chances to develop their debating and presentational skills, and so on. Children in private education are less prone to becoming 'lost in the system'. Nevertheless, I want to stress my personal faith in the state system's ability to deliver a first-class education and to allow children to go on to develop their full potential in any field they choose. It worked for me!

The flip side of giving children the opportunity to discover where their strengths lie is our inherent tendency to decide, far too quickly, that we are not good at certain things. To decide that we're 'not athletic', or 'not good at maths or science'. In reality, most people have the ability to develop a huge range of skills if they put their mind to it, but as people move through their second decade they tend, for understandable reasons, to choose what they think will deliver the best result: the sports they are naturally good at, the subjects that they have the best chance of achieving good grades in that will offer them the best career opportunities or the apprenticeship that suits their skills that will lead to a good career path.

The major drivers in this decade are the education we receive, the extent to which we are encouraged or discouraged from pursuing certain interests and, in a very general sense, the resources that are devoted to helping us develop and flourish.

Different cultures around the world have radically different approaches to the different generations. In some cultures, typically in the East, children are expected to look after the older generation, both physically and financially. The younger generation acts as carers and pension providers for the oldest generation. In other cultures, young people grow up with a sense of guilt about all the things their parents might have done if they hadn't taken on the responsibility of raising children, forgetting that children are not simply a 'financial drain' on their parents and bring other, non-financial benefits with them!

There are some key psychological dynamics at play in all cultures. Most parents hope to give their children opportunities that were not available to them and for their children to take advantage of those and go on to become more successful and wealthier than their parents. Parents, naturally, are a huge influence on our choices in this decade, in one way or another. Some parents steer their children towards careers similar to their own. They have done well in their chosen profession – perhaps law, or medicine, or in management of large corporations – and they feel confident this will offer a good career for their children. Some parents are very aspirational for their children to have more successful careers than their own. They may feel they have worked hard all their lives without becoming wealthy, so they hope their children will be brain surgeons or barristers. And, of course, some children rebel against all of this and set out deliberately to do whatever their parents don't want them to do.

Interestingly, there is a growing number of children who cannot imagine themselves achieving more than their parents, because their parents are as successful as anyone can hope to be. These children are brought up with everything they could possibly wish for – the high school student who drives a Mercedes, for example – and they struggle to become independent of their family. This is understandable and it can be entirely practical: the 'family firm' offers excellent opportunities that may not be easily available on the open market. Some children of wealthy families take the opportunity to work in music, drama or the arts – careers that would normally be seen as financially risky – because they have the 'insurance policy' of their family's wealth.

Most parents look back at this time and think that they were either too demanding and proscriptive about their children's choices or too easy-going; they wish they had pushed their children harder to achieve something the children were reluctant to do but that the parent was convinced they could excel at. It's a difficult balance.

In my experience, if young people have been given enough 'resources' by their education and a supportive, nurturing family background, they can make a success of whatever they turn their hand to. The most important thing is to love what you do. The old quote, "Find a job you love, and you'll never have to work a day in your life," still offers good advice. I have known many people who have become wealthy doing what they loved, even though their chosen profession is not a typical route to wealth. I know wealthy personal trainers; wealthy scaffolders; wealthy social media influencers. If you have drive and passion and you love what you do, you can turn it into a success story.

The best advice for people between the ages of 10 and 20 is probably to avoid sticking with what comes easily or naturally to them. Our early years should be a time of risk and experimentation; for trying out the things that we've always wanted to do but felt we would never be able to do. Even if those things don't turn out to be what we devote the rest of life to, exploring them teaches us new skills and gives us more insight into what we are truly passionate about.

From 20 to 30

Our twenties are the decade when we first move into the real world. We leave education or training and get our first jobs. Some people now leave school, apprenticeship or training at 18, get a job in the post room of a large organisation and rise through the ranks to become CEO – but that's not a typical career path! In many cases, our first job defines, or at least heavily influences, the rest of our careers. This is clearly true for the professions: if you set out on a career as a solicitor, or an engineer or a teacher, you are highly likely to continue on that career path. But it is also true that if your first job happens to be in sales and marketing, or in retail, or in the travel industry, you are very likely to stay in that field. It is important to try to avoid simple inertia and to assess constantly whether a career is giving you what you want. Some people knowingly choose a career that they believe will give them security and deliver a reliable income. They might feel that it is not the most exciting career in the world, but they have taken account of that. Other people may regret that they didn't choose a career that would allow them to travel the world, learn new skills, or explore their creativity. Others simply succumb to inertia: they fail to make the difficult decisions needed to set off in entirely new directions.

It is important to get as clear an idea as possible of the fundamental things that matter most to you, and to take a clear-eyed view as to whether the career you are embarked on can deliver that. Many people allow their education to define them – but you can have a degree in history, for example, and go on to be an astronaut or a football coach. Education teaches us to acquire knowledge and learn how to organise that knowledge and apply it. This is a skill that is applicable throughout life in a multitude of different situations. Companies in general employ people for their ability to assess situations and make decisions that lead to good outcomes, rather than for the precise skillset they have aged 20.

In the same way, it is vitally important to look out for every opportunity to learn new skills and acquire new knowledge. Invest in yourself. If your company offers training opportunities to advance your career, take them. If it doesn't, devote your own time and money to gaining new skills you believe will help you achieve what you want. As with the previous decade, this is a time for experimentation when we should take risks, make mistakes and learn from them. These experiments are all lessons in life, and every lesson can be a step towards success. Some mistakes are very expensive, and the lessons cost a lot. Others cost very little. People who make more mistakes early in life tend to go on to higher levels of success because they get an understanding of what went wrong in previous situations and why, and they build on their new awareness. It is very much like the process of evolution: successful species adapt better to their environment and thrive; less successful species die out. Fortunately, we are able to change our behaviours and develop new life strategies based on what we have learned from our environment. The popular saying, "What doesn't kill you makes you stronger" is very applicable at this stage of our lives.

Some people begin working full time at 18, but most people will earn their first wages in their twenties and discover what it's like to be earning their own money and spending it as they please. Anyone earning over the current threshold of £10,000 p.a. will be automatically enrolled in their workplace pension, which all employers must offer by law. It can be hard to see the benefits of contributing to a pension when you are younger: retirement seems an unimaginable way off and there are plenty of other things you would like to spend your money on! But, as with savings, pension contributions are hugely important for building up future wealth, and there are benefits in terms of tax relief: money you would have paid to the government in tax is put towards your pension instead. We will talk about all these crucial issues throughout the book.

This is also the decade when people are likely to start borrowing for the first time in their life, other than the student loans used to pay for their further education. People may take out a personal loan to buy a car, and they will almost certainly be offered their first credit card. Having a credit card makes you feel well-off, because you can go out and immediately buy things that you want. Sadly, of course, having debt also affects our cashflow. Our monthly disposable income starts to go down, and we now have an obligation to service the debt we have taken on, which can limit our options. It makes it less easy to leave our jobs, for example, as we need to keep earning to pay our increasing commitments. Welcome to the adult world!

At this stage of our lives, having a nice place of our own to live in becomes very significant. The desire to experience complete freedom to grow into ourselves and establish our own autonomy is incredibly morish. Young people are staying in the family home for longer than in previous eras, and many share flats or houses with friends for several years when they first start working. But everyone dreams of their own place to live. Because of the constant growth in property prices, which shows no sign of stopping in the long term despite occasional downturns, owning property is the essential first step onto the 'property ladder', which is another key way of building wealth.

This is also a time when we get the chance to discover our key interests outside of work: the way we most like to spend our time and money when we are not working. This is a vital element in the more general goal of getting a good understanding of what we want from our careers and life in general. It gives us a proper idea of what the ideal 'work-life balance' would look like for us.

Unfortunately, with this growing adventurousness outside the more regulated environment of school or university come additional risks: this is a decade when we are likely to get our first injuries. Most people, because they are young, recover from these very quickly. But some other aspects of young life, like combining risky activities such as driving with drinking alcohol, can lead to major injuries or even death. Even highly responsible young adults can have accidents caused by the irresponsible behaviour of others. Few of us get through the decade without knowing about some young person who suffers a significant and possibly life-changing accident, even if we are lucky enough to avoid them ourselves.

A final thought: as we start to earn money and acquire things, we inevitably start comparing our situation with other people. It is very easy to become jealous of a friend or a colleague who seems to be earning much more money than us. It is worth considering why this is the case: have they made a different career choice? Have they been given a promotion we have missed out on? Perhaps you want to seriously consider a change of career, or perhaps you can learn lessons from why this person was promoted and whether there is anything you can do to put yourself in a position to get the next opportunity for promotion. If you feel you are being wrongly overlooked for promotion for reasons beyond your control, consider moving to a different employer. Making 'tactical' career moves to take advantage of new opportunities and keep increasing one's salary can be a very good strategy for developing your career at this stage.

Be slightly wary of people you know who claim to have made a lot of money from some 'brilliant' investment – typically, in recent years, in technology giants or in crypto currencies. We'll talk about investment in a later chapter. Investments are an excellent way to build long-term wealth, but the supposedly amazing success stories tend to come from whatever is 'booming' at the moment, which recently has been tech and indeed, crypto currency. Both of those markets are entering an inevitable period of adjustment. Some people do make money in boom times, but some also lose a great deal. One sound piece of advice: when anyone tells you that any particular market 'can only go up', be very wary. Once a lot of people come to believe that is true, it is very likely to be the moment when values start to fall, or even crash. Also remember that people tend to present a rosy picture of their lives to the outside world. Other people's salaries are not always as good as they are made to sound. Big investment gains they may have made at some point are not always kept in the long term.

From 30 to 40

We talked about career development in the previous decade. The years between 30 and 40 are where this takes centre stage for most people. I'd like to talk at this stage about a 'growth mentality', which I believe is crucial to success at every stage in life, but perhaps especially in this decade.

The opposite of a growth mentality, for me, is not the absence of growth; very few people don't want to grow and improve in life in some way. For me, the opposite of a growth mentality is perfectionism. I see far more people who are held back by perfectionism than I do people who lack a growth mentality. Perfectionism holds people back because it leads to a state of mind where it's not worth doing anything unless it can be perfect. It's not worth trying to achieve something because they feel they're not capable of doing that thing perfectly, so they don't try.

Some people believe in perfectionism, but it's a falsity; a prison of the mind. Things are always evolving, changing, and moving. What's 'perfect' today won't be perfect tomorrow. Once we understand and accept that, perfectionism tends to fade away because it's irrelevant. It doesn't mean anything. And we start to accept that we can only give something our best shot; we can only try, and accept the risk of failure.

I talk to people about practising courage. Whenever we train our minds or our bodies, we need to practice courage. In an ideal world, you should aim to stretch yourself by only 2% to 3% outside your comfort zone. We should take the same approach to courage, building our courage like a muscle, so that it becomes stronger and is ready when we need it. It's a process of continuous improvement, and it's OK to feel that we're not there yet, as long as we are building our courage and our skills and abilities, little by little.

We understand this better in the physical world. We know that you don't go to the gym for just one session and walk out twice as strong. You have to go to the gym regularly, as often as you can, and then you slowly begin to see improvements. You feel better; you get stronger; after a month or two you can actually see improved muscle development. It's the same with the mental courage to take on new challenges.

Perhaps you feel that you're not ready for that next step up at work. But remind yourself of the skills you already have and of your ability to learn quickly. Throw your hat into the ring, because how hard can it be? If we say we can't do something, because we've never done it before, and we're not ready, we're not perfect, we will never take any chances. I find that once people truly adopt the growth mentality and try to make small but steady improvements to their courage and to their skillsets, they can suddenly accelerate. Because nobody is perfect. Everyone who is successful is pushing themselves beyond their limits and taking on challenges they're not certain they are ready for yet.

Interestingly, it is also worth making an assessment of whether your place of work has a growth mentality or is locked in a fixed mindset, worrying about perfection. An organisation that is hungry for growth and willing to take risks is far more likely to create exciting new opportunities for its employees to grow and develop than a company that is locked in a fixed mindset and won't try anything new until it feels it is perfectly prepared.

In our thirties, we are likely to be married, own property and have a mortgage. We may have additional borrowings for things like cars and house extensions. We have taken on more responsibilities at work and may well be managing a team of people. This is probably the decade where we experience more change than at any time since we left education and first started work. There is also a realisation that this is the decade in which we need to achieve certain things because the time will come when we are not rising stars anymore. We're not bright young things. We are moving on to a phase where people start to wonder why we haven't achieved more and start to think that perhaps we're not up to the challenge.

For people who want to start a family, there is the added pressure of biological clocks ticking. It is increasingly possible to have children in later years, but that may involve the expense of fertility treatments and mean that you will be bringing up young children at a time when you are approaching middle age. Medical advances and the fact that we are staying fit and healthy for longer will undoubtedly push back the age at which it is possible to have children, but for couples who have not yet had children but would like to, this is an important factor in this decade.

People whose children are of school age may be considering whether to send them to private schools, which is a major financial commitment.

For some people, their thirties are the period when they

really 'go for it' in career terms, and work to maximise their earning potential. This may mean acquiring new qualifications and skills; it will certainly mean a great deal of hard work and the ability to leverage all the assets you have - status, networks of relationships, the quality of your work - in order to drive your career onwards. This is a phase where people have a better understanding of their market value in career terms and try to make sure that they are realising their full potential in terms of earning power. There may be benefits in re-skilling or gaining additional qualifications to ensure that the skills and knowledge we have are still those in most demand.

This can be the period when people opt for self-employment and the opportunity to be their own boss and take charge of their own fortunes. They know the work they are capable of doing and begin to wonder if they should keep doing that work for someone else, or for themselves. Again, there is a growing realisation of clocks ticking and time running out: if they don't do it now, will they be able to do it in the next decade? These significant changes, such as sending children to private school or setting up in business on your own, usually involve sacrifices in the form of cutting back on expenditure: fewer holidays and trips to the theatre; no new kitchen for several years. Setting up one's own business can mean raising capital by means of a second mortgage on the family home.

This is also a time of life, sadly, where the first divorces happen. Couples who met when they were young and got married in their twenties can find that they have changed significantly in the last 10 years. Relationships that seemed perfect in the more hedonistic days of our twenties come under strain as the realities of a more mature lifestyle come to bear. On a far more positive note, the 30s are a time when many people get married (even if not for the first time!) These major potential life changes – marriage; children; property; home improvements – all need significant finance. Having built up a cushion of savings in earlier life is a huge benefit at this stage. Most people, however, find themselves giving up something at this age in order to be able to afford something else they feel is more important. Many things may have to be sacrificed to fund the deposit on a mortgage, a new baby, a loft conversion, or private education for growing kids...

From 40 to 50

We talk about 'mid-life crises' for a good reason. As people enter this decade, it is twenty years or more since they started their first careers. It is a time when most of us begin to think about whether we have achieved the things we hoped to achieve when we were in our early twenties. There is also a sense of time ticking away: if we are lucky, we will still be healthy and strong in this decade, but there is a nagging feeling that perhaps we won't be able to take on some new challenge when we are in our fifties and sixties and this is the time to be bold, because it may soon be too late.

People who had children when they were in their twenties will see their children growing up and heading off to further education or their first jobs. It can, unfortunately, be a time when people whose relationships have been under strain and who have been staying together primarily for the sake of the children, decide it is time to end the relationship and move on. For others, having their children move away from home creates more time and space for reflection and a new sense of energy and the impetus to explore new things. Some people take the opportunity to relocate, moving to a different area and finding pleasure in the new experiences this provides: different countryside, new restaurants and shops to go to, new walks to explore, new friends to be made. The increased possibility of working from home, without the need for a daily trip to a central office has made this an even more popular option.

This can be a time when we look for a change of career. Our work has become very familiar; we find it easy because we are so practised at it, and it is not providing us with significant new challenges. People who have established themselves in successful careers may be reluctant to take the risks involved in a move to something new. They may decide that they will stick with it for 15 years before they can retire. Life at work becomes a bit tedious, and they look for stimulation in their outside interests, putting their energy into hobbies, holidays and other pursuits. Other people decide the time has come for a change of career. They may reskill and move in new directions; downsize their lives so that they can support a new lifestyle from a less well-rewarded job, or even move to a different country. For others, this is 'make or break' time, and they decide to take a major risk to achieve something they have always wanted to achieve – perhaps starting their own business or moving into a consultancy role and becoming self-employed. This can be a decade when people find themselves made redundant by their employer, which forces their hand. Nobody wants to be made redundant and, if it happens, it is always a difficult time in people's careers. Nevertheless, several clients have told me that redundancy forced them onto a path that they have since found very rewarding – enough cash from their redundancy payment to give them a breathing space and the opportunity to reassess their career options and, in many cases, to decide to start some kind of enterprise of their own.

By this decade, people have generally built up a certain level of wealth in the form of savings and the value of their property and have a greater sense of confidence in the value of their skills and knowledge. They feel they have some financial buffers in place to ease the blow if something goes wrong and they have options open to them if their previous employment comes to an end.

From 50 to 60

This is the period where people really begin to see the value of financial independence. Most people, by this point, will have a very clear idea of the point at which they can hope to become financially independent. We will talk more about this later in the book, but the concept is very simple in practice - it means you have accumulated enough assets in the form of savings, pension funds and the value of your property to be able to live at some level of comfort for the rest of your life without needing to work anymore. We all have to achieve financial independence by the time we retire, so the interesting question is always exactly when we can become independent and stop work.

Most people take out the first mortgage in their 20s, and the typical repayment mortgage has a 25-year life, so by the time we have reached our 50s, the mortgage will probably be on the point of coming to an end, unless perhaps we have extended the period of the loan when we took out some extra borrowing at an earlier point. Children will be growing up - even for people who have a child when they are in their forties - and the costs of supporting them will be reducing, even if there are still ongoing costs in the form of help with the deposit on children's first property or with covering some of the costs of a wedding. Many people will have built enough savings via ISAs and other forms of saving to fund these costs. In general, there is less requirement to sustain the same level of income and less pressure for people to keep working at the same level and pace.

Some people, at this point, may continue to keep working at their current job because they still find it rewarding. Some may opt for shorter working hours, if that is an option - perhaps working three or four days per week. Some may move into a new role which is less demanding and stressful. Others may take the opportunity to do something creative they have always dreamed of, or to 'give back' via some kind of voluntary work or a move into a role that they feel has more purpose and makes more of a contribution to society in some way.

As the possibility of full financial independence gets closer, some people find this quite tantalising and frustrating: they simply want to reach the end point and retire. They might decide to use some of the wealth they have built up in ISAs, pensions, rental properties or equity in their main residence to provide the final amount of capital needed. Downsizing to a smaller property might be a useful option though people sometimes struggle with that option at this stage of their lives because they have an emotional attachment to the property they live in, perhaps because that is where the children grew up and it is filled with happy memories. They may also be reluctant to leave areas where they have many social connections and close community ties.

These days, as everyone is living longer, people in their 50s are likely to find themselves becoming part of 'sandwich generation.' Their children have not yet become fully independent, and their parents are aging and beginning to need a level of care and support. They are 'sandwiched' between two sets of dependants. There may be new care costs if parents begin to lose the ability to live independently. There may be a need to travel more if their parents live in a different part of the country and they need to visit them more often.

People who have not built up enough savings and other assets in earlier decades may now find themselves playing catch up. One of this book's most important messages is the need to start saving money and building wealth as early as possible. If we start saving early in life, we benefit from the effects of compound interest - earning interest on top of interest as the years go by. The effect is really transformative. If we only start to put money aside late in life, this effect is much weakened.

Everyone's goal, in my recommendation, should be for financial independence by the end of this decade. Becoming mortgage-free is very liberating. It should then be possible to fund a decent lifestyle from the wealth you have accumulated, without having to work anymore. There might be some choices to be made – perhaps forgoing a holiday or some new purchases in return for earlier independence – but once people become financially independent, they can relax and move calmly on to the next period of their lives. They are 'heavily de-risked', as the financial jargon puts it, and have the freedom to enjoy life to the full.

From 60 to 70

This is normally anyone's period of peak wealth, after which they will begin to 'decumulate', spending or gifting the wealth they have built up. Our continuing health begins to become a significant factor and may have an influence on our decisions.

Everyone at this stage of their life will have someone close to them who dies: parents and other family members will reach the end of their lives; friends may suffer heart attacks, strokes or cancer. The more fortunate carry on.

This is a good decade in which to tick off any remaining items on the bucket list of things you want to do or achieve! This is still a good decade to travel, though you probably want to do it in more style than in your earlier life; backpacking is probably off the agenda. If you have any health conditions, health insurance can become considerably more expensive and become a factor. If you have always dreamed of retiring overseas, this is the stage at which you may make a final decision. Sometimes the idea becomes more and more daunting, and the pull of familiarity and security becomes stronger, especially in health matters. But this is still a decade in which new adventures are entirely possible.

People at this time of life may look back and wish they had done more. Perhaps some items on the bucket list will never get ticked but, generally, there is a peace of mind that comes with knowing that you are able to fund the ongoing lifestyle that you want, and that you can begin to wind down.

The arrival of grandchildren can have a big impact and provide a new energy for many people. It may also provide a new job! Many grandparents willingly help with babysitting, childcare, and even doing the school run again, taking the strain off their sons and daughters and helping them get on with their careers. It can be exhausting, but also highly rewarding.

Staying active in this period of our lives is a recipe for a longer life. Regular and relatively light exercise is usually the ideal: walking; golf; yoga – whatever you enjoy that keeps you active. Do as many of the things that you still enjoy for as long as you can do them.

From 70 to 80

This is a real wind-down period. It is a phase when people tend to do a lot more tax planning, thinking about inheritance tax and other issues to maximise the wealth they can pass on to the next generation. Gifting money becomes a very interesting option. Anything gifted within seven years of your death is still subject to inheritance tax, though money that is given regularly and can be shown to be excess income – money that you do not need for normal living expenses – is also free from tax. We will talk about these issues in detail in later chapters on tax and other topics – but there is every chance that money gifted in this decade will remain tax free and will bring a great deal of pleasure to all parties concerned.

If you know that your grandchildren or your children have a key passion in life, you could help them to explore and enjoy it. If they like history, take them to the Colosseum in Rome; if they are interested in music, take them to concerts, perhaps abroad. Your family may protest and say that you should spend the money on yourself, but you can truthfully argue that you are spending it on yourself and getting even more enjoyment because you are doing these things with the family.

These days, many people in the 70s are very fit and active and much the same physically as they were in their sixties, but reaching the age of 75 is a milestone for many people. By that age, you have probably done most of the travelling you hoped to do in your life, are quite likely to be in good physical health but likely to be slowing down and keen to do more of the things you enjoy and as few as possible of the things that you don't enjoy. Your discretionary spend will probably go down quite significantly; people often spend one third less at this time of their lives than they did earlier. People tend to simplify their lives at this point, selling down assets, consolidating and simplifying their financial affairs and leaving more time for the activities they enjoy.

80 and beyond

Our ongoing health tends to dictate many things from the age of 80 onwards. Many people downsize at this point of their lives, perhaps moving into a bungalow or some kind of assisted housing. Most people will have stopped driving by this stage, so it becomes increasingly important to have essential amenities available within walking distance, or within an easy journey by public transport, if possible.

We will talk more about care in older age in a later chapter, but many of us will find that we welcome some form of care in our own home ('domiciliary care') to help us with daily living if we become a little frail – or we may welcome the security of living in assisted housing facilities, knowing that various services are easily available and that there is 24-hour emergency care on call. Domiciliary care can usually be funded from our otherwise reduced normal discretionary spending, and moving into assisted housing or some other more convenient and smaller property is usually funded by selling our previous main residence and freeing up capital to supply our ongoing needs. Residential and nursing care is the most expensive option, but the great majority of people are likely to need this for only a short period at the end of their lives - an average of eighteen months. It is very expensive, but the cost is usually absorbed by the value of our assets at this point in our lives and still leaves a healthy inheritance to pass on.

If we have not already done so, it is essential at this stage of our lives to make a Will and whatever arrangements we choose to reduce inheritance tax on our estate. It is actually far preferable to write our will far earlier in our lives - perhaps in our fifties or sixties - because dying unexpectedly without a Will (dying 'intestate') makes life difficult for our dependents and means that our estate is divided up according to intestacy rules rather than following our personal wishes. We will talk more about both Wills and inheritance tax in later chapters.

It is important to try to live somewhere that is easy for friends and family to visit. With the best will in the world, people will find it hard to find time in their busy lives to travel long distances to stay in touch, and those visits become hugely important to us.

With a 1 in 4 chance of making it to the age of 100 and receipt of a letter from the King, genetics and health will dictate the later years for all of us but the older you get the greater clarity you have on how much you need and how to spend it.

Screenshot from ONS website

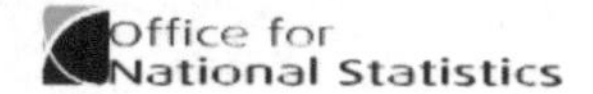

Life expectancy calculator

People are living longer. Improved working conditions, reduced smoking rates and improved healthcare have all contributed to increasing life expectancy from generation to generation.

Enter your age and sex in our calculator to find out your life expectancy, and the likelihood of you living to be 100 years old.

Age

[-] [0] [+]

Sex

[Male] [Female]

Calculate your life expectancy

Your average life expectancy is 88 years

However there's a chance you might live longer...

97 years 1 in 4 chance

101 years 1 in 10 chance

100 years 14.2% chance

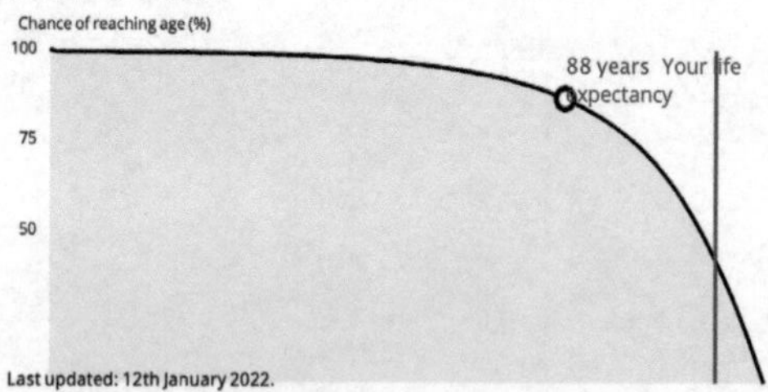

Last updated: 12th January 2022.

Related

Past and projected period and cohort life tables

Statistical bulletin | Released on 12 January 2022

Life expectancy (e_x), probability of dying (q_x) and number of persons surviving (l_x) from the period and cohort life tables, using past and projected mortality data from the 2020-based interim national population projections (NPPs), for the UK and constituent countries

Part II

Chapter 1: Careers and Purpose

Our ability to earn money is what facilitates all our financial affairs and allows us to have the lifestyle we want and to build wealth. Fortunately for most of us, **the things we most enjoy doing** are the things we are good at and, as a result, somebody is likely to pay us for doing them! People who love teaching make great teachers and their career in the teaching profession tends to go well. People who love working with figures make great accountants or finance managers, and the same applies. Non-academic or highly practical people often prefer hands-on work and so may find the trades or physical roles offer greater success.

In an ideal world, our job provides us with a sense of **purpose** and a reason to get up every day and get stuck in. The average span of a working life across the EU is currently 36 years: 38 years for men and 33 years for women, who are likely to take a career break to have children. One of the key themes of the book has been to remind ourselves that we change over time and our wants and needs are very different at **different stages** of our life. The old system of starting work with an employer after leaving school or university and staying with them for the whole of our working life is long gone. There are many more **career opportunities** available to all of us.

One thing I would say is that it is well worth really taking stock and reviewing your career every 10 years or so. The fact that you find it fulfilling and you are successful at it doesn't mean you have to keep doing the same thing for the whole of your life. I have one client who has made a point of making a quite dramatic change of career every 10 years. She effectively wants to live 'more than one life' and so builds in and plans for these changes. She finds that this has given her new challenges and new horizons and kept her stimulated and engaged throughout her working life. That may be a bit too dramatic for some of us, but it is very important to **review our careers** at regular intervals to make sure we are still enjoying ourselves and, equally importantly, to make sure we are being properly rewarded for what we do. We tend to be a bit reticent in this country about how much money we earn. In America, in sharp contrast, people tend to ask even casual acquaintances how much they earn very early in the conversation! It is a very good idea to ask your colleagues what they are earning, to get an indication of comparable salary levels. Services like Glassdoor, which provides company reviews and details of real salary levels supplied anonymously by current and former employees, can be very useful tools. Never be afraid to ask for a pay rise if you feel undervalued at work. I would also advise talking to a recruitment consultant at regular intervals to make sure you are not missing out on other, better-paid opportunities. Some companies offer well-being programmes, better flexibility, remote work, compressed hours or higher benefits. All of these things are part of your compensation, and the value is different for everybody, so it's important to understand what is out there and what works best for you.

There is always a **trade-off** to be made between maximising your earnings potential and enjoying what you do, but having a 'growth mentality' will stand you in very good stead financially. Try to make sure your career is always moving forward and your salary increases are outstripping inflation. If your pay rise only matches the rate of inflation, you will only be able to maintain your current lifestyle. A simple strategy is to try to achieve regular promotions with significant pay increases that will allow you to improve your lifestyle and put money aside to start building wealth.

We talked earlier about how advantageous it is to automate certain behaviours: to regularly put money into savings, for example, so we don't have to make a conscious effort. In just the same way, it is an excellent habit to put more money aside every time you get a pay rise. If you put an additional **1% of your salary** into your pension every time you get an increase, for example, you will be delighted by the results over a relatively short timeframe. You are already getting more money than you had before, so adding this extra money into your pension is something you won't necessarily feel the pain of. It's a very simple way of ensuring you create more wealth for your retirement. Even if you do nothing else than save regularly and boost your savings every time you get a pay rise, the effect of compound interest on these savings will definitely make you better off at retirement.

Most people are employed rather than self-employed (80% of the current workforce) so their employers decide on the value of their pay rises. One of the best ways to make ourselves more valuable to our employers is through **education.** Even though a higher education is no longer the sure-fire guarantee of a successful career that it perhaps was some years ago, government figures still show that working-age graduates earn £10,000 per year more than non-graduates and have higher employment rates.[2] Some fields of study, such as law, computer sciences or biotechnology, are highly likely to lead to well-rewarded careers. Acquiring any kind of **professional skill** gives you an advantage in the job market. If you come to realise, perhaps quite early in your working life, that a particular skill or qualification would make a big difference to your earning potential, it is worth taking time out of your career, if necessary, to get that qualification or acquire that skill. You may 'go backwards' for a year or so while you are studying or training, but you will then have 20 or more years of earning at a higher

[2] Graduates continue to benefit with higher earnings - GOV.UK (www.gov.uk)

level in front of you. Many employers will offer 'on the job' training or can be persuaded to do so – it makes you a more valuable employee, after all. It is always worth pursuing every opportunity to gain new skills in this way. If you can demonstrate a business case for upscaling your skills and align your goals to the company's, they will see this as an investment instead of a cost. Your newly acquired skills will then create new opportunities for wage growth for the rest of your career.

It is worth remembering that jobs in **different sectors** can have different **reward structures.** Public sector jobs such as those in teaching, the National Health Service, the Civil Service or academia tend to offer better pensions than the private sector (final salary pension schemes and 25-30% employer contributions, for example) and may come with other benefits such as higher job security, death in service payments to a spouse, better sick pay and maternity or paternity leave (perhaps 6 months full pay and 6 months half pay, for example) and so on. Some jobs in the private sector pay higher salaries but offer little else. You are well rewarded for that you do, but there is little in the way of other perks, so you have to fund and arrange these yourself! Being **self-employed** appeals to many people (20% of the current workforce) and is increasingly common, but it is very important to build up your own **emergency fund** and **pension fund** from your earnings, because no one else will be looking out for you if you fall ill or when the time comes for you to retire.

Some jobs – perhaps especially senior executive roles in large corporations – can offer the best of both worlds: very high salaries, the opportunity to climb the career ladder plus excellent benefits. If you are working in the corporate world, it is worth paying a great deal of attention to **career progression,** because the rewards improve exponentially as you get closer to the top of the hierarchy. Don't make the mistake of assuming that your employer will always reward your talents with promotion. A corporation's priority is always business success first and foremost, and if you are doing a very valuable job in your current role, they may be content to leave you there. Keep an eye out for every opportunity for promotion and do whatever manoeuvring you can to put yourself in the frame. I have talked with a number of clients who look back on their careers and feel they could have done more to push their career and their salary further at certain key points in their life. It is important to remember that you have more control over this than you may realise. Employers are very loath to lose talented people and can usually be persuaded to push them forward for promotion or to simply improve their salary. There are always plenty of other career options open to you if your current employer is proving inflexible.

A **strategic career move** to a new employer can often be very effective. I have clients who left their company for a better role due to a current promotional ceiling, only to move back to their original company a little later, with a better CV, into a more senior role at a higher salary. The entrepreneur and business magnate Sir Richard Branson once said that if someone offers you an amazing opportunity, but you are not sure you can do it, **say yes anyway** - you can always learn how to do it once you have the new role!

Referencing Sir Richard Branson offers a useful context to qualify my earlier point about acquiring as much education and as many skills as you can to improve your earning capability. Branson left school at the age of 16 with few educational qualifications to launch Student magazine. The magazine wasn't a huge success, but it helped him to launch a record store that developed into Virgin Music. He went on to launch the airline Virgin Atlantic and become a hugely **successful entrepreneur.** His dyslexia gave him problems with spelling and with memorising the information needed to pass examinations that he says still restrict him in certain areas. In a 2019 blog offering advice to UK students who were about to receive their A Level results, he said, "I realised my strengths lay in creative thinking, looking at the big picture, my people-skills, problem-solving ability and not being afraid to say 'yes'. Have a think about what you are interested in and what you are good at – and focus on this."[3]

People who become seriously wealthy often succeed because of their **drive, creativity and energy** rather than

[3] My career was my education | Virgin

because of any particular qualifications. It is also true that owning your own business is often a good route to considerable wealth – the only real rival probably being senior executives of corporations who are rewarded, in effect, with a share of the organization's profits (which they help to create) in the form of salary, targeted bonuses, shares and share options. This is especially the case if the company is a startup or a young venture that subsequently 'goes public', launching its shares on the stock market. In my experience, entrepreneurs can create wealth in literally any field of business – what matters is having the drive to succeed, the stomach for risk-taking and a capacity for hard work. Most entrepreneurs work incredibly hard at key points of their lives and can go literally broke at least once in their lifetime. For these entrepreneurs, any mistakes made are seen as lessons rather than failures, making them better in the future and driving even greater success.

In most careers, people start off using some practical skill they have, such as video editing, writing computer code or being good at marketing but, as their career progresses, they tend to become more involved in **management** skills: working with people, reorganising business processes, restructuring organisations and the like. These roles become increasingly **stressful** and this is often why they are paid more. Senior executives are highly rewarded because they help deliver good financial results for their organisation and build successful businesses, but also because of the toll the work takes on their time, health, comfort and social relationships. It can be very hard to maintain a healthy work-life balance in these kinds of role and many people go through a period of considerable personal sacrifice in the course of their career.

As you earn more money, it becomes increasingly important to consider the effect of taxation on your **take home pay.** It can be quite disheartening to realise that your exciting new pay rise does not actually translate into a great deal of money in your pocket. As you earn money it is taxed in bands. In this example I'll use the 2023-24 tax year amounts, which of course will change over time. You receive your personal tax-free allowance first (£12,570), so £1000 earned equals £1000 in your bank account. We all then pay a basic rate of tax on the next band of earnings (£37,700). This is when National Insurance (NI) contributions at 12% are taken into account and basic rate taxpayers pay 20% income tax, so for every £1,000 extra they might be awarded in a pay rise, their take home is approximately **£680.** Earnings above this level are taxed at the higher rate which increases to 40%, but the NI contribution is reduced to 2% on all earnings above this threshold. Higher rate taxpayers take home around **£580** of every additional £1,000 they earn. Once higher rate taxpayers earn more than £100,000, they begin to lose their initial personal tax allowance on the 'taper' system that we will talk about in the later chapter on Tax, so that for every £1,000 earned between £100,000 and £125,000 they will take home only around **£380.** Once people earn more than £125,140 (as of the tax year 2023-24) they become additional rate taxpayers, paying the highest tax rate of 45% and an NI contribution of 2%, with no tax-free personal allowance, and will take home around **£530** of every £1,000. This is why higher earners expect substantial pay rises to make them feel better off in reality; a very large amount of any extra money they are offered is swallowed up in taxes. This is why putting more money into your pension fund is a no brainer at this level of earnings. You get to keep more of the money you earn.

Some people devote the early part of their careers to stressful but highly rewarded roles, fully intending to make enough money to become **financially independent** and then **switch to a different role**, doing something they have always wanted to do or feel strongly about. We will talk more about becoming financially independent in the chapter on Goals. People might move into something more creative, for example, or work for a charity or explore their love of fine wines and their fascination with the winemaking process. They might start their own business, not necessarily in the expectation of becoming rich, but because they simply want to create and run their own small business and see it succeed. Often the skills they have picked up in the early, highly stressful part of their career allow them to live a more comfortable life offering consultancy services, or perhaps move to a different country where those skills are especially highly valued and rewarded. This can apply to very different career paths: someone might join the armed forces early in life, and then use the skills they have acquired in a highly paid role in the private sector, perhaps as an engineer or a security advisor. Others might acquire teaching skills and then find well-paid work teaching English as a foreign language somewhere else in the world.

For most of us, work is an important and rewarding part of our lives, and something we devote a considerable amount of our time and energy to. For some people, their career is their vocation and their calling. Even when we genuinely love what we do, it is worth reminding ourselves that our career is also a means to an end. We have ambitions for what we want to achieve in our lives outside of work and the kind of lifestyle we aspire to, and our careers enable these. Many of my older clients tell me that they wish, with hindsight, that they had been more **adventurous** in their career, tried more enjoyable things and explored more options in the course of their lives. If your career is giving you purpose – if it is one of the most significant and rewarding aspects of your life – then keep on doing it! Otherwise, regularly review your lifestyle and the finances you need to achieve the lifestyle you want, now and in the future. With good planning, you are likely to reach a point where your finances are secure, and you could make a career move that keeps your finances on track while providing you with a great deal of new satisfaction and reward. If you feel trapped in a career that you are finding stressful and unrewarding, consider very carefully whether the financial rewards are worth it, and whether another career option could provide you with a better balance between work and the rest of your life goals. There are always **choices** to be made and our future really does lie in our own hands.

Shortcuts

- Your power to earn is the thing most likely to make you richer & people do best in careers they love; we tend to get **rewarded most** for **what we do best.**

- It is always advisable to **compare your salary** with peers and industry norms; never be shy about asking for a salary increase.

- Always save **some of the increase** from any pay rise; increasing **pension** contributions by **1%** every time you get a pay increase will help automate **building wealth.**

- **Education, training, increased responsibility, and**

professional qualifications all increase our **earning potential;** taking **time out** to get new qualifications will be repaid through higher future earnings. Seek ways for your employer to invest in your development so that you both get a positive return.

- Different sectors of employment have **different reward structures** and offer benefits other than headline salary, such as job security or higher pension contributions. Consider which is more important to you at different times of life.

- People who are **self-employed** must ensure they are **saving** money for an emergency fund to cover ill health etc and that they are building up their **pension.** Too many rely on the business for everything.

- Pay attention to **career progression** and take **active steps** to move your career forward with your current employer or elsewhere if the road ahead becomes blocked. It is easy to stay too long in one role.

- When someone offers you a great opportunity, **say yes anyway** and work out how to do it afterwards! You then get paid more to practice it.

- A major route to **significant wealth** lies through the success of **businesses;** you might consider starting your own business or working your way up into a role that is rewarded by the success of the company.

- All **management** roles involve doing less of the job that got you there in the first place and more of dealing with people and are inherently **stressful**; you might consider moving to a different career path after a long period of high stress.

- Once you have some level of **financial independence,** you could move to something less well paid that you find very **fulfilling and rewarding** in different ways.

- If you hate your job, consider a change. Ask yourself 2 questions, how do I get paid to do what I love? What would I do if I knew I couldn't fail? You are unlikely to be as successful in a job you resent as opposed to one that you enjoy.

- Your career path is largely a matter of **choice**; your life is in your own hands.

Chapter 2: Savings

Savings represent personal finances at their simplest. You know what you consume (spend) in the course of a week, or a month, or a year, and the rest you can put aside for a rainy day. Even animals do this. Squirrels bury nuts to keep them going through the winter months when food is scarce. Bears gorge on salmon to pile on weight that will last them through the months of hibernation.

What animals don't get, however, is the benefit of compound returns!

Compound interest is a wonderful thing that can help change people's lives. If you put £100 into a savings account with a very modest rate of 2% interest, after 10 years it is worth £121.90. After 20 years, it is worth nearly £150. After 35 years, it is worth over £200. The money has doubled, simply because it was put to one side and compound interest did the rest.

At better rates of interest, things get even more exciting very quickly. At a 5% rate of interest, £100 is worth £162.89 in 10 years, over £265 in 20 years and over £550 in 35 years: the money has more than quintupled.

At 10%...

Let's just say that's why people get excited about getting a 10% return in their capital which, except in times of exceptionally high interest rates, is the kind of return one can only hope for from investments rather than savings. We'll talk about investments in a later chapter. The idea of compound interest is best thought of as someone working for you night and day and you receive the fruits of their labour in the form of returns.

Compounding is the idea of growth upon growth upon growth: exponential growth. The effect becomes more obvious over longer time periods. After 100 years of investment at 5% compound interest, your initial £100 savings would be worth over £13,000. Albert Einstein reputedly called compound interest "the eighth wonder of the world"!

At the heart of the concept of saving is the discipline of taking a piece of what you have and putting it away for later. That simple act is the key to building wealth, being able to buy the things you want in life, retiring early – if that is what you want to do – and being able to do the things you want. Having savings can allow you to make a significant career shift at some point in your life, such as starting your own business or taking an initial drop in salary to follow some new career path. Or taking a sabbatical from work to travel the world...

Start young

Encouraging children to get into the habit of saving is one of the best things a parent can do for them. Children have the same tax-free allowances that adults have, which means they have their own **personal tax-free allowance** (£12,570 p.a. at the time of writing), plus the **starting savings allowance** of £5,000, which is designed to allow low earners to make money from interest on savings without having to pay tax, plus the **personal savings allowance** of £1,000 in interest which is available to all non or basic rate taxpayers. This means a child – like any adult – can earn £18,570 p.a. in interest and any small earnings they may make as they get older before having to pay tax. It is not always necessary to worry about opening tax-free accounts such as Individual Savings Accounts (ISAs) for children, because their total income from interest and any other source of earnings is unlikely to exceed these personal allowances. However, we'll talk more about ISAs later in this chapter, because they can be valuable for sheltering savings from tax if you are putting aside substantial amounts over a long period.

Savings accounts for children tend to have slightly higher interest rates than adult accounts, because banks and building societies are keen to attract clients from an early age. If your parents set up a savings account for you with a particular financial institution when you are young, it is highly likely you will continue to use that account for the rest of your life. These accounts often come with some kind of savings book or the online equivalent to make it a playful activity and give the child a physical sense of their savings getting bigger over time.

One final thought. A lot of people accumulate some sort of savings in their childhood, from their own efforts or from parents putting money aside for them – but they often stop saving in their 20s when they may not be earning that high a salary and there are lots of exciting things to spend money on. The 20s can be a 'lost decade' in terms of savings, which misses out on 10 years of potential compound interest. Saving money as a young adult can make a big difference to people's wealth in their later lives. If they can cement the behaviour of being able to put even a little bit away in this period, it can have a big effect. If they can persist with the good behaviours they saw when their parents were putting money aside for them in their childhood and continue to do even a small amount of regular saving, it creates significant long-term benefits. It's harder to get back into the habit of saving once you stop, and if you maintain even a small element of saving, it never becomes a difficult thing to save in the future.

Variable and fixed rates

When people save money with any kind of financial institution, the institution uses that accumulated capital to lend to other people. If you want to be able to access your money at any time with an **instant access account**, that makes life more difficult for the financial institution because they must have more capital available at short notice and they can't make as many long-term investments. As a result, you will always be rewarded for leaving your money with them for longer periods.

Any instant access account will offer a variable rate of interest that goes up or down typically with the Bank of England base rate. Financial institutions set their own **standard variable rate**, tied to the Bank of England base rate, and that rate will reflect the institution's commercial strategy: whether or not they feel the need to encourage people to invest with them by offering higher rates of interest or think that people have enough incentive to save at lower rates.

It is very easy to shop around and see the various savings rates on offer in the market, but they don't vary a great deal. Building Societies tend to offer slightly higher interest rates than banks because they are set up to provide benefits to their members, whereas banks are listed companies that have to give good returns to their shareholders. But in every case, putting your money into a savings account for a fixed term rather than with instant access will give you a better rate of return. A useful way of thinking about instant access accounts is that you are paying for that access: the fact that you are not committing that money for a longer period costs you money in the form of interest earned.

You don't have to lock your money away for a year or more, though you will be rewarded with a better interest rate if you do. You can get advantageous interest rates for **fixed terms** of anything over one month. The most popular accounts tend to be three months to one year. Two-year and three-year terms offer higher rates of reward, of course, as do deals that ask for various minimum levels of investment. The longer the timeframe over which you're willing to put money away and the greater the amount you are able to commit at the outset, the greater the reward.

It's very useful to decide whether you really do need instant access to your money, or whether you could manage with a longer or short delay.

Emergency savings

Savings that you keep available in the short term via instant access accounts should be seen as your emergency fund. I'm going to offer a valuable rule of thumb.

Everybody should have an emergency fund of three to six months' worth of their normal expenditure.

This is a very good 'golden rule'. Some people might want to have higher amounts available, because they are naturally cautious or because they know they have some big expenditures due in the near future. But the general rule of thumb is three to six months of expenditure, or whatever amount makes you feel secure, so that you don't have to worry about having cash immediately available if you need it.

Interestingly, the older we get, the higher the amount people tend to want to have readily available. It's quite common to see people with £50,000 or even £100,000 in instant access accounts, even though there is little chance of their needing that much cash immediately available in any likely scenario. I find that the amount people have available in instant access tends to reflect their age. People aged 40, if they are in a partnership, tend to have £40,000 available: around £20,000 each. For a couple in their 50's, it tends to be £50,000 in total; in their 60s it's £60,000, and so on. Other factors do come into play as people get older. For example, they might keep some money available if they're going to gift it to children in the near future. But these amounts of instant access savings for older people are almost certainly too high. It is very unlikely that a couple in their 60s really need £60,000 instantly available for emergencies. At this stage of their lives, they are highly likely to have built up wealth in other forms, such as pension funds, and they are likely to be on the verge of receiving a guaranteed income in the form of pensions from those funds and additionally from the state, so that they don't need to worry about unexpected periods of unemployment or sickness. When we're younger, of course, we tend to live for the day and let tomorrow take care of itself! But in general, the golden rule is sound: at any stage of life, have between three- and six-months' normal expenditure saved up and readily available for emergencies. Anything more should almost certainly be kept in a fixed-term account where it earns more interest.

Peace of mind is very important, of course, and people often tell me that they have large amounts of money saved in instant access accounts for exactly that: peace of mind. They feel their money is always available if they need it. But I like to sit down with people and say, "Okay, tell me all the things that you worry about that you might need money for." When you go through that process of thinking about all the things that might require instant access to money, you typically find the list is not that long. People might say that they need a new roof for their house at some point, and we talk about what that might cost. Or they might want a new car. We think about how much they might get for selling their current car and how much extra they might need for something new. Then again, a lot of people tend to buy their cars using finance rather than savings. Perhaps they need a new boiler or would like to redecorate the house. The next questions are: "Are you really going to need a new roof in the next six months? Will you use your savings to buy a new car, or will you use finance? Does the boiler definitely need replacing in the next six months or could it wait longer? Are you definitely going to redecorate?" And the answer is usually, "Well, probably not all of those things and not in the next few months." In general, we find at the end of this process that around three to six months of normal expenditure really is enough for their likely emergencies. The figure works across nearly all levels of income: when we are earning more money, our roofs, cars and boilers tend to cost more, so whatever your level of income, the golden rule of three to six months' normal expenditure for your emergency savings works well.

There is also the possibility, of course, of some dramatic change to our circumstances: people might lose their job, or their business might fail if they are running their own business, and of course anyone may fall ill. These episodes are very painful, but most people find they are back earning some kind of income within six months, so the golden rule still holds. Being out of work for whatever reason, including illness, for longer than six months is unusual, but of course it can happen. Insurance policies covering this kind of eventuality can offer further peace of mind. We will talk about insurance in another chapter; insurance is a more appropriate form of protection against relatively unlikely events, rather than trying to keep enough money in savings to cover every possible eventuality.

Instant access money is for emergency funds and short term planned capital expenditure. Once you go above the amount of money you feel you need for genuine and likely emergencies and things you know you are going to spend money on, such as home improvements, that money should be in a fixed term account earning you a higher rate of interest.

Regular saver accounts

It's worth saying a few words about monthly saver accounts or 'regular saving accounts', which are the entry point to saving for many people. Saving any money – putting aside money you don't need right now – is the key to starting to build wealth. But a word of caution: monthly savings accounts tend to offer a relatively high rate of interest that looks attractive at face value. But only your first month of savings will achieve that rate of interest across the whole year, whereas your last month of savings will only achieve 1/12th of that interest rate, because the money has only been in the account for one month. Interest is typically paid annually, and the real rate of return that you end up getting – the actual interest that's added to the balance across the whole year – is typically half the apparently attractive headline rate and about the same, in general, as an instant access account, if you were to put the money aside as a lump sum. The rate of interest offered is limited to a fixed term of typically 12 months. There will also be limitations on the maximum amount you can save and possibly on the withdrawals you can make. You may need to have an existing current account with the institution offering the regular savings account.

Regular saver accounts encourage us to start the good behaviour of putting aside money that we don't need for our day-to-day needs, which is a wonderful thing, but if you are able to put away a lump sum from the outset, it immediately starts to earn interest on the full amount. My advice is to **do both.** Save whatever you can on a regular basis, because this effectively 'automates' the process of saving. You set it up once, and then you can forget about it – you don't have to keep making a conscious decision to put some money aside. If you come into some money as a result of a bonus at work or the sale of something or an inheritance or whatever it might be, put as much as you can spare into the most appropriate savings account.

Monthly income

Savings are primarily a way to **build wealth.** Once you have accumulated some money, of course, it can also be used to **generate income.** Most banks, if you request it, will pay interest monthly rather than annually. Accounts such as the government-run National Savings and Investments (NS&I) Income Bonds also pay out monthly interest. Everything in NS&I is 100% guaranteed by the government. Their Income Bonds are an instant access account that allows you to invest anything from £500 to £1 million and receive interest monthly for investments locked into accounts on a one-, two-, three-, or five-year term, at increasing rates of interest. They tend to be preferred by people with a very low tolerance to risk. Unfortunately, this kind of investment will **not keep pace with inflation.** Inflation will start to erode the value of the income every year. In the first year, you will receive the headline rate of interest, but every year thereafter the real rate of return will decrease as inflation goes up. Your invested capital will never increase, because you have bought a guaranteed government bond, but your real income will erode more or less quickly, depending on the current rate of inflation.

There are times in one's life when it is useful to take interest as income but, of course, this loses the benefits of compound interest: instead of the interest earned adding to your capital and earning you even more interest in subsequent years, your capital remains the same and the value of your income is eaten away by inflation.

Inflation

Inflation exists in every modern economy. A moderate level of inflation is seen by most economists as being healthy for the economy as a whole. In 2022-23, there were exceptionally high rates of inflation around the world as a result of economies coming back to life after the COVID-19 pandemic, combined with the effect of the war in Ukraine on energy prices.

High levels of inflation are always damaging. So-called 'runaway' inflation can destroy economies, devaluing national currencies until they become almost worthless. There are cautionary tales from around the world and over history of people rushing to spend their weekly or monthly salaries the moment they are paid, because the money will be able to buy less one day later or sometimes even a few hours later. This is one of the worst effects of rampant inflation: it destroys everyone's incentive to save or to invest. People are quickly reduced to living in a barter economy, where they will only sell goods in return for something that has an obvious value: I give you corn from my field in return for milk from your cow. It works, but it is extremely limiting as an economic system. But for stable economies in normal times, inflation tends to be around 2%-3%.

It is vitally important to ensure that **savings are outpacing inflation**, otherwise the benefits of compound interest are lost. Interest rates have been exceptionally low since the financial crisis of 2008 as central banks tried to stimulate the economy by reducing the cost of borrowing to almost zero. At times of high inflation, banks typically raise interest rates to encourage people to save money rather than spend it, so the return on savings improves but, again, it is essential to keep track of whether your savings are increasing in real terms when the effect of inflation is taken into effect. At times when interest rates have been historically low it is also worth considering whether it is wise to put money into longer-term fixed-rate savings accounts, because of the risk of locking away money at low interest rates at a time when inflation may start to rise. Remember that, in any case, savings should only be kept for 'emergency' use; any money that can be put aside for longer periods – more than five years, for example – should be kept in investments, which have a far better record of significantly outperforming inflation in the longer term.

Risk

Risk is an important factor in everyone's savings and investments decisions. Many people keep money in lower-interest-paying instant access accounts because they feel their money is safe there and they can always get at it in a crisis. It is true that there is some risk inherent in absolutely every form of saving and investment: nothing is risk free; even large financial institutions can go bust. In the global financial crisis of 2008, the UK government had to step in to rescue the Northern Rock bank. The government also intervened to support RBS (previously known as The Royal Bank of Scotland), Lloyds Banking Group and Bradford & Bingley. These were extraordinary events that no one had foreseen.

However, as a direct result of that crisis, financial institutions were forced by the government to increase their resilience to financial shocks by increasing their capital and liquidity buffers, and today's financial institutions are safer for investors than ever.

In addition, **the UK's Financial Services Compensation Act (FSCA) guarantees £85,000 of savings per individual** across a wide range of financial institutions, provided the institutions have been authorised by the Financial Conduct Authority (FCA), an independent public body, or the Prudential Regulation Authority (PRA), which is part of the Bank of England.

If a financial institution goes bust, people's savings are covered up to this amount. **Married couples** are protected for £85,000 each, a total of **£170,000.** Many people spread their savings across six or seven different bank accounts or savings accounts because they feel this is reducing their 'risk', when in fact this is unnecessary because of the guarantee by the FSCA. Spreading savings across many accounts in this way is time consuming and harder to keep track of; better to choose a few favoured accounts for different purposes - instant access, 6-month term, 3-year term, for example - and concentrate your money in those.

There is another caveat that really only applies if you have higher levels of savings: the £85,000 per person guarantee covers a financial institution and **all of its subsidiaries,** so if you have several investments amounting to more than £85,000 in various institutions that are all subsidiaries of one larger institution, your cover might be less than you imagine and it would be worth double checking who owns which institutions.

There is one final aspect of the FSCA scheme that I find many people are not aware of: consumers are covered for up to a **£1 million pounds for what are called Temporary High Balances that result from major life events.** If you have an unusually large amount of money in an institution as a result of a house sale, a redundancy, divorce, inheritance or some form of compensation, you are covered for up to £1 million for **six months** after the money arrives in your account.

ISAs, Premium Bonds and tax

An ISA is effectively a tax-free wrapper. The government allows you to save a certain amount per annum **free of income tax.** You can save currently £20,000 per person per year in an ISA without having to pay any tax on the interest.

Bear in mind, as we saw earlier, that you can earn £1,000 in interest tax-free (£500 for higher-rate and zero for additional rate taxpayers), and when interest rates are low, there may not be any immediate benefit in putting your savings into an ISA. If interest rates are 2%, for example, and you save £20,000, your interest earnings will be £400 p.a., and no tax will be payable. In this scenario, you are better off simply looking for the best interest rate available on the market, which are often not in ISA accounts. However, savings put into ISAs each year are sheltered from income tax forever, so if you know you can make regular savings year after year, ISAs can be advantageous – every year's savings within an ISA are **sheltered from income tax forever.**

There are various kinds of ISA. The **Cash ISA** is just like a regular savings account with a tax-free wrapper. With **Stocks and Shares ISAs** money you save is put into various investments chosen either by you personally or, if you prefer, by a fund manager, who will charge a fee, and **earnings and capital gains** from your investments are both tax free. If you are looking at saving in an ISA over a 5-year period or longer, it is worth looking at a Stocks and Shares ISA.

Wealth built up in ISAs is **not free of inheritance tax.** ISAs can be a great means to build wealth and to spend your money in your lifetime, but an ISA on death is just as useless as everything else! There is one exception: investments made within a Stocks and Shares ISA in the Alternative Investment market (AIM) are exempt from inheritance tax if they are kept for two years or longer. AIM is a part of the London Stock Exchange which specialises in smaller companies and applies a lighter regulatory regime than that which applies to larger, more established companies launching on the main market. AIM investments are very volatile and you should always seek advice before considering an investment, but in later years of life they may be worth considering within an ISA because of the exemption from inheritance tax. We will talk more about AIM investments in the chapter on Tax.

If you are married, **your spouse will inherit your ISA allowance.** If you have built up let's say £100,000 in ISAs during your lifetime, in the year of your death your spouse's ISA normal £20,000 annual allowance will be increased by that amount so that they can move the inherited ISA into their own ISA. This one-off increase is known as the Additional Permitted Subscription (APS) allowance.

For anyone aged between 18 and 39, the **Lifetime ISA** can be a useful way to build up funds for a house purchase or for retirement, because the government contributes to your savings. You can currently save up to £4,000 per year (which counts towards your total £20,000 annual ISA allowance). The government then contributes 25%, so your £4,000 becomes £5,000. If you are saving towards buying a house, you must be a first-time buyer, and the maximum value of the house you can buy is currently set at £450,000. If you are saving for your retirement, you can only pay in until you are 50 years old and you cannot withdraw the money until you are 60. Any other withdrawal faces a 25% penalty. The 25% is applied to your initial savings plus the government's 25% contribution so the penalty does not, sadly, simply take back the government's contribution. For example, if you save £1,000 and the government contributes £250, you now have £1,250. 25% of that is £312.50 – more than the government's £250 contribution. In addition, you lose any tax relief on the money you withdraw.

Banks are apparently finding these Lifetime ISA accounts burdensome because of the complications involved in working with the tax system and, and they have not been taken up by that many people, so there is a chance that these ISAs will not stand the test of time and may be withdrawn from the market by some institutions.

Junior ISAs are a popular way of saving for a child. You can save up to £9,000 a year into a Junior ISA on behalf of a child and build up a useful tax-free sum to which they will have access when they are 18 years old. Again, if you are planning to save over a long term – perhaps the whole 18 years of a child's life until the money becomes theirs – then, as we said earlier with regard to longer-term ISA savings, you might consider the stocks and shares Junior ISA rather than a cash Junior ISA.

There is one more form of tax-free saving that is well worth mentioning: NS&I **Premium Bonds** can be a useful option for many people. Premium Bonds are a kind of national lottery bond. They were first issued in 1956 by the UK government. You can buy a maximum of 50,000 £1 Premium Bonds per person. Every £1 bond has an equal chance of winning, so the more bonds you have, the higher the odds of winning. There is a maximum £1 million prize, which is awarded two times per month, then there are other cash prizes from £25 (over 2.5 million awarded per month) to £100,000 (56 per month). The annual prize rate is currently set at 3% of the fund's value, which suggests that you might hope to see a 3% return on your investment – but that isn't the case. If you held the maximum bonds worth £50,000, the likely average return in prizes in any one year is £1,000 or 2%. Of course, you might win nothing at all, or £25, or £1 million! But, on average, you can hope to see a return of maybe 2% at current prize rates. The good news is that your capital is guaranteed by the government and all winnings are free of income tax, so Premium Bonds can be a useful and sensible place to hold some emergency savings, especially if you are a higher rate taxpayer or an additional rate taxpayer. There is, of course, still the risk that typical levels of winnings from Premium Bonds may not keep pace with inflation.

A final note: if you are a higher rate taxpayer or an additional rate taxpayer but your partner is a basic rate taxpayer, it may be worth **holding some of your savings in your spouse's name** in any particular tax year. As we saw earlier, every basic rate taxpayer has their personal tax-free allowance (currently £12,570 p.a.), plus the starting savings allowance of £5,000 p.a., plus the personal savings allowance of £1,000 p.a., so they are able to earn a total of £18,570 p.a. before any tax is due.

Trusts

People who are building up substantial savings on behalf of a child are often understandably nervous about the child getting access to that money at the age of 18, in which case some form of trust may be advisable! When an adult sets up any kind of savings account in a child's name, such as a Junior ISA, they are effectively acting as a 'trustee' on that child's behalf, but in those case, the savings will be automatically transferred into an adult ISA account when the child reaches 18, and the trusteeship comes to an end.

Having a large amount of money put aside in a child's name outside of vehicles such as Junior ISAs can have significant tax implications. If you save in a child's name as parents outside of an ISA and the money makes more than £100 in interest or any other kind of investment return, that money is taxed as if it was your own income under what is known as the **parental settlement rule.** Grandparents and friends can gift as much as they like in a child's name and the child will not incur any tax on that money, but that too can have tax implications for the person making the gift. The government is very wary of gifts that have the effect of moving money around without it having the opportunity to tax that money!

Creating a trust with the child or children as beneficiaries avoids the parental settlement rule. Trusts can have multiple trustees, so that if anything happens to one trustee, there is someone else who can taking over the running of the trust. The trustees decide when to allocate money to children and for what purpose, following the instructions set out in what is called a **Letter of Wishes**, which might stipulate that money is to be used for a child's education, or to buy a first property, or becomes available when the child reaches a certain age, etc.

The psychology of saving

This may seem a strange thing to say in a chapter extolling the benefits of saving, but some people do get a kind of **addiction to saving**, and they save more money than they actually need. The point of saving is to build up enough money to buy things that you want, or to have enough money put aside to be able to stop working and retire early. Some people build up substantial savings, which gives them a feeling of security, but when they think about taking some money out and spending it – on that holiday of a lifetime, for example – they feel they will become less secure. There is a psychological barrier between saving and spending. Every time you look at your balance it keeps getting bigger and bigger and bigger, you feel warmer and cosier and more secure. It becomes a bit like body armour. People think, "No matter what happens, I'm fine. I've got my savings to fall back on," and the idea of actually spending those savings makes them feel fearful and less secure. This can be problematic for some people. They go past the point where that money is useful. It's become a kind of crutch, and they're so fearful of spending it and becoming poorer, they never get to enjoy the benefit of what they've saved up for in the first place.

It is incredibly important to remember that **the only point of saving money is for it to be spent on the things you want,** which includes gifts and inheritances to your loved ones. There are also the possible expenses of long-term care in the case of illness, which is something we will talk about in a later chapter. But it is possible to hang on to too much money out of a mistaken sense of security, and to miss out on some of the good things in life that the money was intended to be used for.

I like to use an analogy with shopping for food. When we buy food, some of it is to be eaten quite quickly: fruit, for example, will go into the fruit bowl to be eaten within days. Some other foods go into the fridge, if they are to be eaten within a week or two. We put some food into the freezer to keep for longer periods. And the point about food, obviously, is that it's there to be eaten. We want to keep it fresh and ready to eat for just as long as we need to. It's the same with savings. Instant access savings are available for immediate use – for 'emergencies.' Other savings, like fixed-term savings and money saved in ISAs, are like food in the fridge: put aside for a little longer. Anything longer-term should not be kept in the form of savings but should be invested in other ways that offer better returns. This is like the food we put into our freezer. I tend to refer to this as 'pension' money: money that is put aside until you need it at some later date. But the food in the freezer is still there to be eaten and the 'pension' money is still there to be used when needed!

Shortcuts:

- **Compound interest** is the eighth wonder of the world. Putting money you can manage without to one side in a savings account allows the wonders of compound interest to **build wealth while you sleep.**

- Starting to save money **at a young age** will help build wealth more quickly. Try to keep saving in your 20s and cement in place a positive habit!

- Build-up & hold between **3- and 6-months'** typical monthly expenditure in instant access savings for **emergencies.**

- Savings for planned spending held **longer than as an emergency fund** should be held in higher-yielding **long-term savings** accounts.

- **Inflation** is the biggest risk to savings: try to ensure that interest earned on savings is higher than inflation. In the longer term, UK savings rates have not always kept pace with inflation.

- The government's various personal and savings

allowances may mean that typical earnings from savings are not taxable until those allowances are surpassed. ISAs and Premium Bonds **shelter savings from tax** and can be very useful but typically pay lower headline rates.

- Be wary of becoming **addicted** to holding money in savings; money saved is money intended to be **spent at some point.**

- Any savings that can be held for periods **longer than 5 years** are likely better held in **investments** rather than cash savings, and my recommendation would always be to **always seek professional advice** before making longer-term investments of this kind.

- Saving this month isn't sacrificing, it is increasing your purchasing power next month. Learn to budget and enjoy saving.

Chapter 3: Debt and Mortgages

When I was younger, I wasn't keen on debt, because my mother was averse to borrowing to fund purchases and would avoid it at all costs – a good example of the way we acquire financial 'habits' early in life without even being aware of it. Now, after years of working in the finance industry, I appreciate the complex and important role that this has in people's lives. Debt allows you to **leverage** a regular income, allowing you to acquire things now by budgeting for them over a period of time. They say that money makes the world go round, and the same is true of debt. Debt oils the wheels of the economy and keeps it moving. If we had to wait until everyone could afford a house, to choose an obvious example, there would be virtually no housing market.

In the late 1950s, households across the UK benefited from a new financial service known as hire purchase, a form of debt. This credit arrangement made it possible for ordinary families to buy washing machines, tumble dryers, refrigerators and televisions – consumer goods we take for granted today and see as 'essentials'. Customers paid for their chosen products over a set number of months or years, with the proviso that they wouldn't technically 'own' them until the final payment had been made.

This was a revolution in personal finance that helped people improve their standards of living. In 1948, only 2% of UK households had a refrigerator. By 1970, the figure was 58%. That wouldn't have been possible without debt in the form of hire purchase. The whole electrical goods sector was essentially built on this form of debt and the idea spread to the purchase of furniture, carpets, cars and almost every kind of major household expenditure. Debt **generates liquidity** in the economy, helping to build businesses and create jobs and wealth.

Debt is simply what you owe, and credit is what you can borrow. Debt helps you to purchase a home of your own (via a mortgage), buy a car (using a loan or finance agreement) and make home improvements or take a well-earned holiday (perhaps via a credit card). The period in our lives when we most need debt is typically between the ages of 18 and 50.

When you take out a debt, you make regular payments to a lender for a fixed period of time, for the privilege of having something today rather than at some point in the future. It's a transaction between you (the customer) and the lender that has benefits for both sides. The lender doesn't personally know you, so they take a risk that you might not repay the debt. The interest charged is the lender's return for the risk they run in lending the money and, of course, for the fact that they are making capital available.

The word 'debt' has both positive and negative connotations, and your attitude to it is largely influenced by what your parents thought about it – as in my own case! If they believed people should live within their means and save up for what they need instead of borrowing money, you are very likely to have the same mindset, at least in early life. If they struggled with money and were often in the red, you are likely to be averse to the idea of getting into debt yourself. On the other hand, if your parents were always able to pay off loans and credit cards, you may see debt for what it is: a way to have what you need or want without having to wait for it, providing you can always afford the repayments and pay it off at the end of the term. You simply budget for it over a fixed period of time. Used wisely, debt can be a tool that can be used as leverage to acquire assets, when the timing is right for you but you don't necessarily have the resources immediately available.

Credit ratings and lending risk

In the so-called Bank of Mum and Dad, parents routinely write off money they lend to their children. Every other lender, unfortunately, has a strictly commercial approach to lending money.

Underpinning everything is the **credit rating** system. This allows lenders to predict your future behaviour by looking at how you've dealt with loans in the past. If you've kept up repayments without any problem and paid off loans or credit agreements, that positive pattern helps to build up a good credit rating. The higher your credit rating, the more banks may lend to you because you have demonstrated your reliability in paying the money back with interest. When you apply for loans, credit cards and mortgages, lenders are more likely to look at your application more favourably.

Missed payments will also appear in your credit history and adversely affect your creditworthiness. Also, if you haven't taken out any credit before, you won't have a credit rating, so it can be difficult for lenders to assess whether you are a good risk. This can seem counterintuitive to many young people, who assume that never having been in debt shows they are good at managing their money. In fact, taking on affordable levels of debt as a young person and always making the necessary repayments helps to **establish a good credit rating** from an early age.

You can see your current credit rating for free via credit reference agencies such as Experian or Equifax, although you'll have to pay a fee if you want to see more detail. It is important to realise there is no one universal rating because the various credit reference agencies calculate them in different ways. There is also no industry-wide 'blacklist'.

It might sound strange, but one of the best ways to build or boost your credit rating is to take out and use a **credit card**, and pay it off in full every month by setting up a direct debit. This will show the lenders in the credit system that when you take out credit, you pay it back. So long as you repay it in full each month then you typically don't pay interest on the debt either.

As well as being good for short-term lending, credit cards are useful for insuring things you buy. If you buy anything that costs more than £100 and less than £30,000, you are covered under the Consumer Rights Act if the item is faulty or damaged, is not delivered, or doesn't match the description, and if the retailer refuses to refund or replace the item. Flights and holidays are also covered, and paying for these by credit card can offer a useful level of insurance against cancellations or airlines and tour operators going bust.

Some credit cards allow you to pay for things in different currencies without incurring fees. Others have cashback elements, 'points' earned with certain retailers, or perhaps Air Miles. If you shop around, you are likely to find something that can be beneficial for you.

Credit cards charge a **higher rate of interest** than almost any other form of debt – an average of **25%-40% Annual Percentage Rate (APR)**. They are designed for short-term credit and should ideally be paid off in full at the end of every month, giving you up to four weeks' free credit. Any debt that stays on a credit card for any length of time is very expensive to service.

So, although paying the full amount of interest owed but not the full amount borrowed will not affect your credit rating – as far as they are concerned, you are still making your commitments – it is a very expensive way of borrowing money.

Credit card companies will routinely offer to increase your credit limit, hoping to encourage you to spend more. Unless you genuinely need the higher credit limit, it is wise to refuse the increase in case you may be tempted to use the additional available credit without having the means to repay the full amount every month.

Debt and credit for young people

The first time many people encounter credit is when they take out a **mobile phone contract.** This is a financial agreement and is a form of debt, though many people don't realise this at first. They have to make the monthly payments without fail. It's important to keep a cap on spending limits on your phone so that you don't exceed them and potentially find yourself unable to pay in any particular month. If you miss a payment, that will go on your credit history and affect your future credit rating.

Most banks will give you an **overdraft** when you first become a customer. Many will offer you an initial **interest-free** overdraft. This is called an **arranged overdraft.** If you go over your overdraft limit or become overdrawn when there is no overdraft arrangement in place, that is known as an **unarranged overdraft**.

In April 2020, new rules for banks were introduced to clamp down on excessive overdraft fees. Since then, the same interest rate must be charged for both arranged and unarranged overdrafts, there are no daily or monthly fees for actually using your overdraft, and interest on overdrafts is charged at a single APR, typically between 19% and 40%. An overdraft, like a credit card, is an expensive way to borrow money and should also only be seen as a short-term temporary measure. Try to avoid going regularly into your overdraft; if you find this happening, it is a sure sign that you are routinely overspending and that it is time to revisit your budgeting. It is also not good for your credit rating.

When you first become a student, you will be offered a **student bank account** which normally also comes with a 0% interest overdraft while you remain a student. If you go over the overdraft limit, you will be charged interest and if you haven't cleared that overdraft by the time you graduate, a higher rate of interest will apply because you are no longer a student. This can come as a shock, but it is also a useful life lesson: 'introductory offers' come to an end, and overdrafts are an expensive way of borrowing money.

Student loans are a special form of loan, first introduced in the 1990/91 academic year to replace student grants. The interest rate on student loans is based on the Retail Price Index (RPI), a measure of inflation. It has recently been capped because of the current high rate of inflation, but the interest rate on most student loans is still relatively high. However, the repayment terms for student loans means that most students will not repay the full amount of the original loan plus interest. At the time of writing, graduates are required to contribute 9% of everything they earn over £27,295 a year towards the debt, for a maximum of 30 years or until their death if they die sooner. In practice, most students, unless they become very high earners, will not repay the full cost of their student loan plus interest incurred over 30 years, and lower-earning graduates will pay relatively little or nothing at all. Some people like to pay off their student loans early - often with help from their family - so that they will be 'debt free', but this is not always financially advantageous in the long term. This is a complex area, and it is worth taking professional advice.

Another common type of loan is the **personal loan**. People often take these out to pay for home improvements, or to buy a new car, pay for a wedding or go on a once-in-a-lifetime holiday. If you have a reasonable credit rating, you are likely to be able to get up to £30,000 as a personal loan relatively comfortably.

The duration ('**term**') of any loan makes a huge difference.

The **longer the term**, the smaller your monthly repayments will be, but **the more interest you will pay in total.** Lenders prefer you to take longer-term loans because they get more of a return in the form of interest payments. Reducing the term will cut down the amount of interest you end up paying – but it is important to make sure that the monthly repayments are comfortably affordable. At some stages of life, it is worth paying more interest over a longer timeframe to ensure that your repayments are manageable.

All of these types of debts – credit cards, personal loans and overdrafts – are **unsecured loans.** That means if you can't pay it back, the lender can't take away any of your possessions to pay for the debt, which means, of course, that these are riskier kinds of loans from the lender's perspective.

Defaulting on debt

The consequences of missing payments on a loan or credit card and going into arrears can be quite serious; this is known as **defaulting** on a debt. If you ignore letters from your lender or if an agreement to pay off the outstanding amount can't be reached, a **County Court Judgment** (CCJ) may be registered against you. The equivalent process in Scotland is known as enforcing a debt by diligence. A CCJ is a court order under which the court will set a schedule of monthly repayments. If you are able to pay off a CCJ within 30 days of the order, it will be removed from your credit file. Otherwise, it will remain there for **six years** and will seriously affect your ability to get future credit – a mortgage, for example. You will be classed as a high-risk borrower and the interest rate on all future debts will reflect this.

If you ever find yourself in a debt crisis, get advice from one of the free debt charities, rather than going straight to a debt management company, as the latter will charge fees. There are several different formal debt solutions in the UK, depending on the amount of debt you have. They include **debt relief orders** (minimal assets process in Scotland); **administration orders; bankruptcy** (sequestration in Scotland); and **individual voluntary arrangements** or **IVAs** (protected trust deeds in Scotland). A debt charity will be able to advise you which one is right for you and your circumstances. Of these, bankruptcy is the most serious outcomes as it has many far-reaching and long-lasting effects on your finances and circumstances.

It is vital to stay in contact with your creditors rather than ignoring the issue and ending up in court. Smaller monthly repayments may be acceptable to them because they would rather receive something than nothing at all. It's also important to seek help as soon as you realise you are struggling with debt, so that events don't spiral out of control and become more difficult to sort out. It is possible to slowly rebuild your credit rating after a debt crisis, even after bankruptcy.

Mortgages

A mortgage is probably one of the most useful forms of debt and the one that most people in their lives will take out, even if they generally avoid debt in other forms.

A mortgage is simply a loan used to purchase a property. It is a **secured loan**, which means that the lender effectively owns your home until the mortgage is paid off. Because the loan is secured, it is less risky for the lender and more affordable for the borrower. If repayments are not kept up, your home can be repossessed and sold to repay the lender's capital.

Most **residential mortgages** are **repayment mortgages** that automatically pay off both the interest and the capital over time. At the end of the mortgage term, borrowers will have paid off the capital they borrowed plus all interest charges and will own their home outright. The maximum term has traditionally been 25 years, though longer terms are now available as demographics and society have changed. Mortgages are now available for terms of up to 40 years. The rate of interest is the same on the debt, but the longer the term, the less capital you pay back each month from the outstanding loan, which is why payments are lower. As with every form of debt, extending the term can make payments more affordable, but will increase the total amount of interest paid over the term of the mortgage. Mortgages are offered at standard variable rates, fixed rates, discount rates or tracker rates, which are explained below.

Some people, especially if they are remortgaging their existing property later in life, may choose to switch to an **interest-only mortgage**, perhaps because they are going through a change of career and would like to reduce their outgoings for a period. Having an interest-only mortgage dramatically reduces the monthly cost of a mortgage, because no repayments of the capital are being made, but the borrower must demonstrate they have a plan in place for repaying the capital at the end of the term. Such repayment vehicles might include ISAs, investments, expected inheritances, or the sale of another property, such as a rental property. This method is typically higher risk because it depends on many variable factors, such as investment performance, tax laws, an inheritance being spent before you actually receive it and the many other variables in life that can't be accounted for. But for some clients, it can work.

When applying for a mortgage, there are three criteria that lenders look at: the amount of deposit you have, your income and that of anyone you apply jointly with, and the affordability of regular repayments.

The more money you can contribute as a **deposit**, the lower the risk to the lender and the better the interest rate you'll be offered. A deposit of 5% or 10% of the value of the property is usually the minimum for most lenders. If you can manage to raise a bigger deposit, your repayments will be lower and more affordable, and your total interest payments over the full term of the mortgage will be less, but with current house prices so high in many areas of the country, raising a large deposit before buying their first property is not an option for many young people.

Lenders refer to the **loan to value (LTV)** ratio of a mortgage, which is simply the proportion of the mortgage compared with the value of your property. For example, if you borrow £225,000 to buy a £250,000 house, your LTV is 90% because you are borrowing 90% of the value of the property. The maximum a lender will offer you is typically 95%.

A mortgage with an LTV of 75% or lower will always offer the lowest interest rates. If a lender has to repossess your property, they will typically only get back 75% of the value of the property when they sell it at auction. LTVs higher than 75% go up in 5% increments – to 80%, 85% and so on – and each increment will come with a higher rate of interest, reflecting the lender's increased risk that they may not recover the full value of their loan if the borrower defaults.

In terms of the amount of money you can borrow, lenders will usually offer around **four and a half times your single income** or your **joint income** if you are applying with a partner or friend. Lenders also have to follow strict rules enforced by the Financial Conduct Authority to check the **affordability** of a mortgage for the borrower. They have to take into account your income and your outgoings, including your other financial commitments, such as a personal loan or other finance if you are buying a car, for example, or any outstanding credit card debt you may have. They will consider whether you could still make your mortgage repayments if the interest rate on your mortgage went up, if you changed career, if you started a family, or if, in the case of joint mortgage, your partner's income was reduced at some point. This is to make sure you don't overstretch yourself and that lenders are only offering an amount that you can comfortably afford to repay. It is always tempting to borrow as much as possible to buy the most desirable property, but it is essential to avoid missing a monthly payment, because of the effect it will have on your credit rating.

If you are buying your first home, remember this is just your first step on the property ladder. You can move on to a larger property in a few years' time when you've built up some **equity** in your home. 'Equity' is a term used to describe the amount of money by which a house's market value exceeds the mortgage on it. If you have a mortgage of £300,000, for example, but the market value of your house is £400,000, you have equity of £100,000. After even a few years of paying your mortgage, your equity will increase as you begin to reduce the outstanding debt, and your property hopefully increases in value with inflation. If you choose to get a new mortgage on your property after a few years, your LTV will be lower, and you may be able to get a lower interest rate. In practice, of course, most people tend to **trade up**, using their growing equity and earning power to buy a larger property. The higher their wages, the more people can afford to pay for more expensive houses. Over the long-term, property will increase by around 4% per annum and so double in value every 15 years but there are always periods of volatility to consider as the market cools and overheats. Lower market valuations typically occur during periods of recession or high interest rates, when the cost of servicing debt is much higher, affordability is constrained and confidence is low in the employment market. Prices will fluctuate by postcode depending on specific local factors such as regeneration projects, gentrification and changes to demand and supply of available housing, but when interest rates are low, the economy is strong, and people are spending money on home improvements, then values will typically increase.

There are a variety of additional costs to factor in when buying a property, such as surveyors' and solicitors' fees, but most first-time buyers are able to avoid stamp duty, which is a tax the government imposes on the purchase of more expensive houses. All properties with a value of £250,000 or less are exempt from stamp duty, and first-time buyers can currently buy a home up to the value of £425,000 without incurring stamp duty.

At the beginning of a repayment mortgage, most of the monthly repayment goes towards paying interest and only a small amount towards reducing the capital borrowed. This balance shifts as the capital is paid off and the interest owed reduces. Over time, people's wages are also likely to increase, and it becomes easier to afford the repayments. Every time you take out a new mortgage, you have the choice to reduce the term, so that the loan will be paid off earlier, or extend it to reduce your monthly payments, which can be useful at different periods of your life. Remember that with a large capital purchase, such as a house, inflation works in your favour. The amount you initially borrow does not increase and is effectively frozen in time, while inflation reduces the real cost of that capital. This is easier to visualise over the long term. There was a time when people could buy houses for £20,000, which was the amount of capital that person would have to repay, plus interest charges, in order to own their home outright. £20,000 today does not seem like a great deal of money, because of the effect of inflation. Even several hundred thousand pounds in 'today's money', will soon be less in real terms, because of the effect of inflation. If your wages increase above inflation and the debt stays the same (i.e. you don't borrow any additional funds), sooner or later you should consider reducing your mortgage term to increase your repayments as they should then be more affordable. This will ensure you are debt free sooner and you also save several years of interest payments. As an example, just remember that for every £100,000 borrowed with an interest rate of, say, 3%, you are paying £3000 in interest each year so if you can reduce your term by just 2 years then that's £6000 saved over the term of the mortgage, which is equivalent to a nice holiday to celebrate when you become mortgage free!

Fixed and variable rates

Lenders will typically offer an incentive in the first few years of the mortgage in order to encourage you to borrow from them. At the end of the agreed beneficial term, the interest rate will switch to the lender's **standard variable rate** which will then vary with the **Bank of England base rate.** This will always be higher and should be avoided as much as possible. At this point, most borrowers shop around to find a new fixed-rate mortgage at the most advantageous rate.

A **fixed rate** mortgage is usually preferable for first-time buyers as well as those who need or like to control their outgoings because it means they will pay the same amount each month for a set period of time, regardless of what happens to the base rate. As a rule of thumb, it pays to lock in a rate for longer periods when interest rates are low, such as 5-year fixed rate deals. When rates are high, a shorter timeframe, such as a 2-year fixed rate deal, may be more suitable, as these will tend to be slightly lower in cost. In my experience, the longer the fixed rate is, the more a lender may add a risk premium as they are effectively taking a risk that rates may go higher or lower than forecast and they will factor this in. Having said this, the typical difference between a 2- and 5-year deal may be as low as 0.2% and as high as 0.5% on average.

A **discount mortgage** offers a discount off the lender's standard variable rate for a fixed period, after which, again, the interest will revert to the lender's standard variable rate.

Tracker mortgages offer a variable interest rate linked to the Bank of England base rate over a longer term. With both discount and tracker mortgages, the rate of interest goes up and down with the base rate. These can be a useful option if it is expected that interest rates may fall in the relatively near future, but this is a difficult forecast to make, and it is wise to take professional advice. Discount and tracker mortgages are useful if you are happy to 'go with flow' of changes to the base rate and have less need to fix your repayments at a precise maximum in the short term.

If you want to pay off the whole of your mortgage while you're still in an incentive period – the period for which the lender has guaranteed a lower rate of interest – you will typically have to pay an **early repayment charge**. This could be anything from 1% to 5% on the whole mortgage and typically varies with the amount of time left in the incentive period. On a five-year fixed deal, for example, the penalty might be 5% in the first year, 4% in the second year, and so on. Because the penalty is payable on the full cost of the mortgage, it can be substantial. A 5% penalty on a £200,000 mortgage, for example, would be £10,000.

It pays to plan ahead if you have a mortgage with a fixed incentive period and start shopping around early to see what is on offer from other lenders. Mortgage offers are valid for a certain period, perhaps as much as six months. You don't have to take up an offer as soon as it is made, and you can hold on to it for those six months knowing you have the option while you keep an eye on interest rates and see if a cheaper option becomes available.

Buying with friends and family

People who are single and struggling to get a sufficiently high mortgage offer on their own salary can consider **buying with a friend**. Clubbing together in this way means you will benefit from offers linked to two or more incomes, just as those with partners or spouses do. If you decide to go down this route, it should be with people you trust implicitly. Remember to talk beforehand about an exit strategy if one of you decides to leave for whatever reason. Unless you can afford to buy out your friend's share of the market or quickly find someone to replace them, you will probably have to sell the property. You may also find yourself paying the full mortgage until a sale is finalised if the friend does not or cannot continue to contribute to their repayments.

Another strategy that parents increasingly use to help their children get on the property ladder is the **family mortgage**. Lenders take into account the parents' income when calculating the mortgage offer and treat the parents as guarantors for the debt, which means it will appear on their credit file. Grandparents can also get involved, but intergenerational mortgages like this are still quite specialist and it would be wise to make use of a mortgage broker.

Overpayments

You can make **overpayments** on most mortgages of up to 10% per annum without any penalty. If you have regular bonuses, you can make one-off payments, or if you get a pay rise, you can increase your direct debit every month to repay your debt earlier. This is always worth considering, if you can afford it, as it will reduce the amount of interest you pay over the full term of the mortgage and allow you to become mortgage free earlier.

Further advances

If you want to borrow more on your existing mortgage, you may be able to get a **further advance.** This is sometimes called a **second charge**: the first loan is guaranteed against the value of your house and any further advance will also be guaranteed by a new, 'second charge' against that value, so that the lender can recover their money by repossessing and selling the property if you default on payments.

Further advances are most often used to pay for a house extension or other improvements. Lenders are usually happy to lend to homeowners for improvement work because this will further increase the value of the property.

Getting a further advance on a mortgage will be the cheapest way to borrow money, but you will have to undertake a new affordability test. Your lender will charge you a higher rate than the first mortgage product you took out, perhaps on a different fixed rate for a different period, so the two mortgages are not aligned. There may well also be an early repayment charge on this second charge also.

When you come to remortgage after taking out a further advance, it is common to combine the two mortgages into one so that the amount you owe and the length of time you're using to pay it off are aligned. This rebalances the debt and should also allow you to find a cheaper overall rate.

Bear in mind that for most residential mortgages, the maximum term is normally capped at retirement age. However, there is now a growing market in mortgages available to **older house buyers**, not least because many people are buying their first property later in life than previously. Borrowers with interest-only mortgages might also find that they do not have enough capital to pay off their mortgage at the end of its term, or they may want to release some equity later in life from a property they by then own outright, in order to make gifts to family members or to make some large expenditure – on home improvements, for example, or the holiday of a lifetime.

Many lenders will allow borrowers to have a mortgage that extends **beyond normal retirement age** (to perhaps 75 or 80) if the borrower is still earning. Any continuing work would need to be 'reasonable' – that it to say, appropriate for the age of the borrower and likely to continue. Other sources of income, such as pensions, investments or rental income would also be considered.

A **Retirement Interest Only (RIO)** mortgage lends money against the value of the property, charges interest only, and reclaims the capital when the owners die or go into long term care and the property is sold by their estate. They are generally available only to borrowers over the age of 50 or 55. Where the mortgage is in joint names, lenders will need to be reassured that the interest payments could continue to be met if one partner were to die – perhaps from a widow's or widower's pension.

Equity release mortgages are available for borrowers over 55 and give borrowers a lump sum guaranteed against the equity they have on the property. As with a RIO mortgage, interest is charged monthly, and the capital is paid on death or when the borrowers go into long-term care. If you can afford to pay the interest payments for the rest of your life, equity release can be a useful way to make money available later in life for various purposes. It means that there will be less money to pass on as inheritance, but for some older borrowers who have in any case built up substantial funds to leave in their estate, the additional mortgage may allow them to retire to a better or more suitable house, paying the interest on the new mortgage from their retirement income.

Some equity release mortgages do not charge monthly interest payments, so that there is no additional ongoing cost to the borrowers themselves, and the interest is 'rolled up' into the capital owed. This is like **compound interest in reverse** – the effects of compounding are now working against you! The original amount borrowed quickly grows, and must be repaid from the proceeds of the eventual sale of the property, greatly reducing the amount of money that can be left as inheritance.

In general, you can borrow more against your property the older you are. Some lenders offer a 'no negative equity guarantee'. This means that the amount they agree to lend will never become more than the value of the property when it is sold. This ensures that your estate will not have to actually repay any money to the lender, even if the amount of interest finally owed is more than the final value of the property.

With a **home reversion plan**, people sell their property or a percentage of their property in return for the right to live there rent free for the rest of their lives. Home reversion companies will typically offer 25% or 50% of the value of a property so if, for example, you sold all of a house worth £400,000 to a Home reversion Company for 50% of its value to raise £200,000, there would be no residual value left to your estate. The house has been sold, so even if the property has gone up in value and is finally worth more than the original valuation of £400,000, that value will belong to the lender. Where only a percentage of the value of the house was sold, there will be a corresponding level of profits left to the estate.

Porting and bridging loans

If you are happy with your existing mortgage, you might be able to transfer it to a new property. This is called **porting**, and it means you won't be subject to any early repayment charges that might otherwise apply. However, you'll have to apply for the option, and you will still have to satisfy affordability criteria. This may be a problem if your circumstances have changed, for example, or if you have higher outgoings or have become self-employed.

Another issue with porting can occur if you need to borrow additional funds. The lender may insist that you take out a separate mortgage product in addition to your existing mortgage, so you could end up with two mortgage products on different rates. It's important to factor in all the associated fees to make sure that porting is the best option before you go ahead. The alternative is to pay off the mortgage with the proceeds from the sale of your property and get a new mortgage for the new property.

When you sell your home and buy another you could find yourself needing to exchange contracts on the place you're buying before you've completed on the house you are selling. In this case, you may need a **bridging loan**. This is a short-term, high-interest loan that 'bridges' the gap in the period when you're waiting for proceeds of the sale. Bridging loans are expensive, with typically high set-up fees and an interest charge of up to 0.5-1% per month. It can be tempting to take out a bridging loan before you have sold your current property if you have found a property you very much want. This is extremely risky, as you cannot be certain how long it will take to sell your property. Ideally, a bridging loan should only be considered once you have exchanged contracts on the sale of your current property, after which the buyer is unable to pull out of the purchase. Bridging loans are also often used for beneficiaries of an estate settling inheritance tax bills as you have to pay the tax to the government before you can have access to the estate.

Offset mortgages

With an **offset mortgage**, your surplus income and any savings are combined into one account along with your mortgage borrowings, though they are kept in separate 'virtual' pots. Your savings and excess income are used to reduce or 'offset' the interest you pay on your mortgage. For example, if your mortgage is £200,000 and you have a positive balance of £20,000, you will only pay interest on £180,000 – the difference between the two figures. This can help you pay your mortgage off earlier because more of your repayments are going towards paying off the capital, rather than interest.

An offset mortgage can be seen as one big overdraft facility, because you have ready access to any money in excess of your mortgage borrowing without having to ask the lender. Offset mortgages can be useful for people with high incomes, regular bonuses or large savings. But they are not suitable for everyone because they have a higher interest rate, which is also always variable. They are perhaps also best avoided by people who would be tempted to spend the 'extra' money available rather than to keep it as long-term savings.

Advantages of offset mortgages

- Any interest you end up not paying because of the offset against your positive cash balance would have been paid out of your taxed income: you effectively pay zero tax on the interest you save.
- You could save more on your interest than you would earn in a savings account, because the interest rate charged on your borrowings is higher than the rate offered on your savings.
- You can still make deposits and take out money from your savings account.
- The reduced interest charges in the long term mean you could clear your mortgage sooner or pay less each month.

Disadvantages of offset mortgages

- Interest rates can be higher than comparable standard repayment mortgages.
- You normally won't earn interest on any cash held in accounts linked to the mortgage.

- If you have savings, you might choose to use them to pay for a bigger deposit on the original mortgage rather than to offset ongoing borrowings.
- There's a relatively small range of offset mortgages to choose from.

Mortgages for second properties

If you want to buy a **second home** or a **holiday home**, lenders will assess the affordability of the new mortgage based on your total outcomings, including of course the mortgage, if any, on your main residence.

You will usually need a minimum of 10% and possibly 20% deposit, which is designed to reduce the lender's LTV risk levels. The interest rate will also be higher because the loans are a greater risk for the lender; if things get tough, lenders consider you are less likely to keep up payments on a mortgage for a second home than you are on your main residence.

Buy-to-let mortgages

A **buy-to-let mortgage** is specifically designed for people who buy property as an investment, either as an individual or within a limited company structure. Buy-to-lets are interesting because they are an example of leverage in action and can be used to grow your wealth.

It is important to remember that property prices do not always go up and that there will be periods when the value of property falls, sometimes dramatically. However, as with other forms of investment, property values in the UK have shown strong growth over the long term. If you purchased a £300,000 property with a £75,000 deposit and a £225,000 buy-to-let mortgage, a growth in value of 4% per year, as an example, would represent a £12,000 increase in the value of your property in one year, for an investment of £75,000. If you are able to build up a portfolio of rental properties, the income can be useful, and the capital gains can be significant.

Buy-to-let mortgages are usually taken out as **interest-only** and there is a minimum deposit of 25% required. The maximum most lenders will offer is primarily based on the extent to which a realistic assessment of monthly rent exceeds the monthly interest repayment: the rental income needs to be at least 125% of the interest-only mortgage repayments and in some cases higher. In addition, lenders will have the usual affordability requirements to make sure that you have not taken on too much debt in total.

Buy-to-lets are a popular way of growing wealth and providing extra income, perhaps for retirement. Most lenders will allow buy-to-let mortgages to extend well past normal retirement age. When mortgages come to the end of their term, the property will need to be re-mortgaged or sold to pay off the mortgage. Saving money into an ISA to help repay the mortgage can be a good idea if you want to avoid having the sell the property at the end of the term.

There are various costs to take into consideration when considering buy-to-let, including stamp duty on the purchase of properties, maintenance fees, buildings and landlords' insurance, agents fees (if you use letting agents) and tax on rental income. There will nearly always be periods when the property is empty when landlords look for new tenants to replace the previous occupants, and mortgage payments will need to be maintained throughout these periods. The government has also recently phased out the relief that was previously given on mortgage interest payments: interest payments for buy-to-let mortgages could previously be set against overall profits, giving higher rate and additional rate taxpayers relief at 40% and 45%, and this is no longer the case: landlords now receive a tax credit on only 20% of their interest payments. This, in particular, has made buy-to-let income relatively **tax inefficient.**

One option is to set up a **limited company** which owns and manages the property, in which case **interest on a mortgage** is allowable as a cost that can be **offset against the company's profits.** However, a corporate borrower is riskier for the lender, because companies can always put themselves into liquidation, leaving the lender with no one to pursue for any losses they may make if the company defaults on the loan and the property has to be repossessed. Mortgage loans to limited companies tend to have higher interest rates as a result.

When you come to sell a property, any profits will be subject to **capital gains tax**, which can be substantial. The capital gain is assessed against income tax bands for the tax year in which the profit is realised, which in many cases will push people's gains for that year into the higher rate tax bracket. Capital gains tax on property is currently 18% for basic rate taxpayers and 28% for higher rate taxpayers. If the capital gain does push your income into the higher tax rate bracket, you will pay tax at 18% on anything that falls below the tax threshold when your regular income is included, while anything that falls above the threshold will be taxed at the higher rate. If you are in any case a higher rate taxpayer, you will pay 28% on the full amount of the capital gain. Money you have spent on improving a property can be set against capital gains tax, but not money spent on maintaining it. Everyone has an annual allowance for the amount of money they may earn in capital gains before paying tax, though this was reduced from £12,300 in the tax year 2022/23 to £6,000 in 2023/34 and £3,000 in 2024/25.

Mortgage brokers and financial advisors

When you are taking out a mortgage or a loan, it is worth considering consulting a mortgage broker or financial advisor. Brokers have access to a wider range of mortgages than are available direct to the general public. They can also talk through your specific requirements and priorities and help you to understand your cashflow and spending. They will help you explore the impact of extending or reducing the term of a mortgage and look perhaps at options for regular or occasional overpayments that suit the pattern of your earnings and outgoings.

Shortcuts

Debt

- **Debt** helps **leverage** our income and allows us to acquire the things we want sooner in life.
- Don't borrow too much on short term debt for short term lifestyle boosting.
- Maintaining a good **credit rating** helps get access to the best offers and interest rates.
- Take on only the level of debt you can **comfortably afford** to repay.
- **Using a credit card and repaying the balance every month** can be a good way to build up a good credit rating.

- **Missing any debt payment** has an adverse effect on your credit rating and will make **future borrowing more difficult and expensive.**

- **Mobile phone contracts are a form of debt**; missing a payment will affect your credit rating.

- **Credit cards and overdrafts are expensive** forms of debt and should be avoided or used only for very short-term borrowing.

- **Defaulting** on a debt can have serious consequences; **talk to your lender,** take advice from freely available debt charities, and do everything possible to come to an arrangement for repayment.

Mortgages

- Mortgage offers depend on **income** (single or joint), **level of deposit, and affordability.**

- **Fixed rate mortgages** give peace of mind that repayments will not increase over the agreed term. Fix for longer terms when rates are low and consider variable rates when they are high.

- **10% Overpayments** are nearly always possible without penalty and will reduce the term of a mortgage and total interest payments.

- A **further advance** on a mortgage for home improvements or other use is likely to be the cheapest way to borrow money.

- It is typically possible to **port** an existing mortgage to a new property rather than incurring exit fees; **bridging loans** can bridge a gap between purchase and sale but are expensive.

- **Inflation erodes all debt** over time in real terms.

- **Mortgage brokers and financial advisors** have access to specialist mortgages that are not available to the general public and can advise on products that best suits individual needs. Let them do the leg work for you to save you time and effort.

- If you take on debt, **insure yourself.**

- Don't overstretch in periods of low interest rates and use the monthly cost saving in lower interest to pay off more capital each month.

- Have a **repayment plan,** ideally set your debts up on a repayment basis to automate this but if you opt for interest only, choose a method which doesn't leave things to chance. Don't hope that you will have the money later.

Chapter 4: Lifestyle

The term 'lifestyle' was coined in 1915 to describe 'a way of living', and what the Oxford English Dictionary described as the 'characteristic manner in which an individual lives his or her life'. The key word here is 'individual' because we are all different. What we like and dislike, and find that we need and don't need, determines our lifestyles. The common factor is how we feel about things. Because we are all so different from one another, only individuals can say if they feel they have a good lifestyle or not.

For most of us, our lifestyle is dictated by how much money we have to spend on the various things we want. The higher our level of income, the greater the lifestyle we can afford.

But not everybody wants an expensive lifestyle – that is not necessarily everybody's key objective. It's fascinating to watch documentaries depicting the lives of people in remote villages in places like Papua New Guinea. The people there don't have Sky TV, a Tesla or any of the modern trappings that may be considered desirable or even necessary in Western society. Their lifestyle is simple, purposeful and often centred around the hunter-gatherer model. Everyone has a job and a place in society: they work hard, rest, play, and go to bed at night when they are tired. Their lives have the same rhythm and their lifestyle centres around family. They are all quite cheerful and happy with each other, and they seem to have everything they need. It shows that we don't necessarily need to own lots of things to be happy.

As individuals, the key point we need to decide is what makes us feel rich or poor, and what makes us happy or not. What do we really enjoy doing? What makes us happy and fulfilled? The most successful people in life work out the answer to these questions early on, but it is easy to be influenced by external influences. Marketeers, in particular, work hard to make us feel that we will only be happy if we have the latest mobile phone or a particular brand of trainers.

Let's take the concept of internal thinking and external thinking, and how it affects us. The idea of internal thinking is that we can be happy at any point in time if we think it and believe it. It's a choice we can make if we choose to. I can give you a very good example of this. Imagine that someone has crashed into your car and damaged it, and that you are understandably very unhappy about this. You are angry, and in a rage. You jump out of your car to confront the other driver. Now imagine that they tell you they were rushing to the nearest hospital because they had gone into labour, or because their mother or father had suffered a stroke or a heart attack. Your anger immediately dissipates. A piece of information – some rational knowledge – has completely changed your mood. which means that your emotions are not something 'beyond your control.'

If people can internally accept that they are happy with a particular standard of living, or with certain things about their lives, then they can be truly content. Friends, family and all the people we meet in our lives might try and tell us we need something different to be happy, but that may be based on ideas about their own happiness, external thinking, or external influences such as social media. And marketeers, obviously, have their own, commercial agenda. External influencers often want us to agree with their choices and recommend doing what they have done to get vindication of their choices. These recommendations rarely put the other person's goals, aspirations or interests first.

The more we work out for ourselves what we most like doing and what makes us content, as opposed to being influenced by these external factors, the better our lives will be. By reflecting on our goals and dreams, and understanding our incomes, spending levels and lifestyles, we can plan how best to get there. Do we want to move to the country, travel the world or be mortgage free as early as possible? Do we want a better work-life balance? If we can understand what lifestyle is best for us as individuals, that will dictate all the numbers and finances needed to achieve it.

Essential spending

Every individual has to cover two main types of spending in life: essential spending and discretionary spending. **Essential spending** covers bills for housing, heat, light, security, utilities, Wi-Fi, insurance, food, drink, day-to-day transport, council tax and housing. Everyone needs a home: a safe environment in which to live. When buying a home, people usually start off with a mortgage, but at some point they will pay off the debt and own their property outright. Some of us might be fortunate enough to inherit a house. Some of us might rent properties all our lives. But having a place to live is the foundation of everything else.

For most people, essential household bills including groceries normally cost about £1,000 a month. This amount can of course be lower or much higher depending on personal tastes. Bigger houses cost more to heat and maintain. Bigger or better versions of everything push the total cost up considerably, like an expanding balloon.

Whether we shop at Waitrose, Whole Foods, Tesco, Home Bargains or Lidl, there is quality in absolutely every single offering. Bigger and better is not necessarily offering the best value; we may just be succumbing to the marketing hype. Having said that, there is evidence from experiments in neuroscience that people's brains react more dramatically when they know they are consuming well-known brands. When they are drinking what they know to be Coca-Cola, for example, all of the associations they have with the brand seem to come into play in their brain, and they seem to 'enjoy' the drink more than when they believe they are drinking some unidentified brand of cola. You probably get a lot more pleasure, in various forms, from wearing a designer watch or a designer outfit than you would from wearing something far less expensive. It's a complex area. Consuming heavily marketed brands or desirable luxury goods can genuinely make us happy. Every individual will see different value in different things.

Discretionary spending

The other form of spending is **discretionary spending,** and covers things we choose to spend our money on because we see them as an important part of our lifestyles.

You can argue that all of these discretionary spends are related to our various **senses.**

Firstly, there's **taste:** the different quality of foods available; buying a daily coffee; what we eat for lunch or dinner and how much that food and drink is savoured and enjoyed. This doesn't apply to everyone. I have met people who don't especially enjoy eating and only see food as essential sustenance. They are happy to live on bread and cheese or the equivalent, and they don't see the point of spending lots of money on food. But for most of us, food and drink are an important part of life's pleasures. For some, they can become very important. Many people spend a lot of their leisure time dining out in restaurants or can find themselves building up collections of their favourite wines and coffee from around the world because they enjoy them so much.

Then there is **smell**: aromas and scents. There is a sense of joy and stimulation if you go somewhere that smells nice. That is why the bakery is often the first thing customers encounter when they walk into a supermarket. Liking the smell of baking bread seems to have been hardwired into all of us over the millennia. Our senses are stimulated, and we immediately feel hungry, enticing us to go further into the shop and start spending. But this isn't just about hunger and food. We avoid 'bad' smells and are drawn to pleasant smells. We are happy to spend our discretionary money on air fresheners and scented candles for the home, or on aftershave or perfume, because smell is important to us. An extreme example was Elton John who famously spends hundreds of thousands of pounds on flowers each year for his houses.

Next, we have **vision and sound**: people love to look at beautiful things and hear beautiful sounds. Nearly all of us spend money on various kinds of decorative items for our homes. High quality paintings and sculptures – 'fine art' – can be seen as delightful but non-essential, but for some people art is genuinely essential in their lives. A serious 'art habit' can be very expensive! In the modern electronic age, high-end televisions and home entertainment systems offer wonderful audio-visual experiences in the comfort of our own homes, though many people prefer to go out to theatres, cinemas, concerts or exhibitions to be part of the experience and to connect with others socially. One of my own big discretionary spends is on music, because it is a real passion of mine. I love going to live concerts and I've also managed to acquire a lovely guitar collection, something that has certainly been worth working for.

Touch is the final sense we can stimulate through our lifestyles. Beautiful fabrics and other materials have a luxurious feel to them that is additional to their beautiful appearance: silk has been prized as a fabric since ancient times. Expensive cars have a wonderful feel in terms of the comfort of their interior and the way their controls respond to our touch.

We all have **hobbies and passions** that enrich our lives and are an important part of our discretionary spending. It could be a season ticket to watch a favourite football club, making our gardens beautiful, learning to cook gourmet-style or enjoying wine-tasting. One of the major things the pandemic taught us is the value of spending time with friends and family. Entertaining and sharing a meal at home need not cost that much, though many people love the social aspect of eating out with friends and making an occasion of it, something they would not want to do without.

Then there are our sports and physical activities. Some of these activities require significant discretionary spending in terms of kit or equipment; others are relatively inexpensive. Going for a walk in the country costs almost nothing!

Travel is an important discretionary spend for most people, and there are different grades of travel because everybody has their price. Let's say you wanted to fly to Thailand. A ticket might cost £5,000 first class; £2,000 business class; and perhaps £700 for economy class. Different people will choose different options. It is perfectly possible to travel on a shoestring and see the world. For others, travelling in style is what brings them the most pleasure.

Learning the ideal level of expenditure that brings us the most reward is hugely important. We tend to assume it all comes down to what people can afford and how much they are willing to work for it, but if someone has a high-paying job and can afford a more luxurious lifestyle, it doesn't necessarily mean that lifestyle will make them happy. Each individual has to make their own choice. One thing that is unavoidably true is that having more money gives you more options!

In 2022, the median income for the average person in full-time employment was £640 a week, or £33,280 a year. After tax, that is just over £2,000 a month. This would cover £1,000 for your essential central bills and £1,000 for discretionary spending (a couple might ideally want £1,000 each). There are a lot of variables to factor in, such as how far people have got in paying off debts, where they live, and so on. But for the majority of us, a satisfactory lifestyle should be within our grasp.

The general principle of **Pareto's Law** applies here, as in many areas of life: the 80/20 rule that says that 80% of outcomes come from 20% of causes.

80% of people's joy will come from 20% of their activities. Finding that 20% is crucial. No one has to choose ten different sports or interests; they might have only two or three favourites. But if they take part in them more often, perhaps increasing the 20% to just 21%, they can make themselves exponentially happier. This is a key concept that many of us never really grasp, but it's actually essential in life. It also applies to reducing those 20% of things that produce 80% of our unhappiness. Simply aim to reduce these 'unhappy' activities or associations by a little. It works brilliantly.

For some people, work is the most important thing in their lives; it's their purpose. But the average person will not identify so closely with work and their personality, traits and lifestyle are reflected more in the things they choose to do outside of work. These are the activities, hobbies and passions that make us most happy, and they are very likely to be what we will do more of when we stop working: work is the means to get us to that point. Generally, the more experiences we have in life, the more lasting memories we will create and the happier we will be. If we have the freedom to use our wealth to increase our day-to-day happiness, the more enriched we will feel. Understanding our lifestyles is key to this.

Seasons of life

It can be helpful to think of the different stages in life in terms of the seasons. It is also useful to think about **value** versus **quality** versus **quantity**, because how we feel about these changes in the different seasons of our life.

During the **spring** season of our lives, from our teenage years up to the age of 25, we tend to be quite frivolous with spending because it is the first time we have had our own money. We are still finding our feet and don't yet understand the lifestyle we want, so we spend on quality and quantity but don't necessarily know the value of things. We live for today and have high levels of discretionary spending – perhaps because most of the essential bills are still covered by our parents.

When people first move into their own place, it tends to be a bit of a wake-up call as they discover how much is needed to cover the essential bills. During this period, they are using their discretionary spending for themselves and/or their partner. And, of course, a significant proportion of our lifestyle in this season of our lives is devoted to finding the right partner!

There is a saying that if you buy cheap, you buy twice. This becomes more relevant as we get older and it is followed by those in our **summer** season between the age of 25 and 50. At this stage of life, we look for higher levels of quality and more consistency of spending. Although we have greater resources, if we have started a family, there will be more mouths to feed. In addition to the essential bills, we may have to factor in paying for childcare, insurance and interest payments on loans for major purchases. As we saw earlier, most of us at this stage of our lives choose to cut back on non-essentials to afford these new expenses. People may also consider private education and private healthcare. Long-term security also becomes more important, so saving remains a vital part of budgeting, and life insurance upgrades may be necessary. Value for money becomes more important.

By the **autumn** phase of 50 and 75, most people know exactly how much they need each month in terms of budget because they know their lifestyle and what they like and don't like. There is less need for experimentation. This can be a **decumulation period** when we might no longer need to save. If debts and the mortgage are paid off, this changes the equation. A tapering off of their lifestyle in some areas also starts to occur in these autumn years. They do not necessarily choose to go out as often or need to do as many things, and their spending changes along with our lifestyle. They might also choose to start giving away a certain proportion of their wealth. If they do choose to spend on new physical things, there tends to be a higher spending threshold because people have more disposable income and can afford more expensive goods. The accent shifts towards quality.

During the **winter** years between 75 and 100, discretionary spending generally drops by a third. Most people will not travel long distances as much, or do as many physical activities, but time with family and friends is paramount. By this age many people will have seen what they want to of the world and they don't feel the need to explore the rest of it. Returning to favourite locations in their lives provides guaranteed enjoyment and minimal disappointment. The bulk of their discretionary spend goes on security and pure comfort as well as quality time together with those they care about. They have already acquired everything they own; they are less likely to be doing big DIY projects or opting for a new sofa. At this age, the mentality is often 'I've got what I've got – it's good enough and it'll see me through'. However, care fees might become a consideration during this phase and gifting excess funds becomes more important and also easier to do.

Lifestyles in retirement

Total discretionary spending for the average couple is likely to be about £2,000 a month. People can do most things they want with that amount in the UK, so it is relatively comfortable. That would cover clubs, hobbies, accessories, clothing, meals out, some wine and drinks and occasional holidays. Anything over and above this level of discretionary spend is approaching four-star- and five-star-style living – which is delightful if you can afford it, but not essential!

There are only so many holidays a person can take when they are still working. Even Generation Z and millennials, who might work more remotely and perhaps have a lower cost of living, are still working for most of the day. In retirement, of course, people can take more holidays. It is often believed that when we are no longer working, we will want to be on holiday all day and every day. The reality is that we like our day-to-day living and sleeping in our own beds, so we do not take as many holidays as people might think. That said, the costs of travel can be reduced in retirement because people can travel when they want and there is no need to travel at peak times and it is possible to benefit from competitive rates. Retirees often travel for longer periods so may have just the same number of holidays, but instead of weekends away they take three weeks – because they can!

The **amount of money we need in retirement** is an all-important number that will inform the choices we make while we are working. One of the best things everyone can do is to work out what kind of lifestyle they need or want and crunch the numbers; they can work back from there to decide exactly how much they need to have to achieve it. A lot of people I talk to find they need less than they had imagined in order to have an adequate savings and pension pot.

As a general rule of thumb, cautious people might draw down and spend around 4% of their liquid assets per year to fund their retirement. The key question is, how long would that last? Let's say you had £1 million saved, which you want to last for 30 years, taking inflation into account. £1 million at 4%, would equate to £40,000 a year, or £3,333 a month. For most people that is plenty. If you only needed £20,000 a year to sustain a satisfactory lifestyle, then taking 4% of a £500,000 pot of investments/pensions would generate that amount.

Typically, investments should produce this 4% annualised return on average over the longer term without eating into your capital, so the money shouldn't run out. However, there is a useful calculation that academics have worked out that represents the safe withdrawal amount for any given period over the last 100 years. It suggests that drawing down an average of 3.1% of total savings in any period of the last 100 years would ensure you would not run out of money. This includes retiring on the day before world wars broke out, or the dot.com bubble burst, or the financial crisis began! If you invest at the start of the recovery, then the safe figure to spend is often much higher. In reality, most people find they draw down small amounts in semi-retirement, more in the early years of full retirement and then less in the later years. Generally speaking, if you get good investment returns early on, then the amount you can spend increases quite dramatically, but if you only ever took 3.1% of your investments each year then this would have kept your capital intact for every period of the last 100 years, even if you had started to draw money down at the start of every market crash, so it is a good figure to bear in mind for those who are really cautious.

If people have less money put aside, they could begin to spend down their capital later in life. Or, if your capital seems to be more than enough for your needs, you could decide to pass it on sooner to the next generation. The point is that it is possible to accumulate too much wealth that will never get spent. If someone has built up too many assets, they will start looking for things to spend their money on. The general principle is that once a person has over liquid £2 million at retirement (typically 50+) to generate an income, that is enough for 99% of people when they own their own house, don't have any debts and will likely get a full state pension. Remember for most people, discretionary spending typically drops by a third from age 75. Very few octogenarians are spending £80-100,000 per annum. In reality, we want to spend more in early retirement when we are fit and healthy and then taper off our spending naturally over time.

Once you have enough to cover your lifestyle, anything over and above tends to get spent on acquiring more assets and can end up going into Brewster's Millions mode. You may have seen the 1985 film of that name. The idea of the film is that the main character can only qualify for an inheritance of $30 million if he spends $3 million within 30 days without acquiring any assets. It's quite hard to spend money and not acquire something – the only way to do it would be to buy experiences (or, in Brewster's case, to spend huge amounts of money or a supposedly doomed political campaign, amongst other things). Funnily enough, acquiring experiences is generally more fun and more memorable than acquiring things. But there are only so many 'once in a lifetime 'experiences one has an appetite for!

When people have millions of pounds in the bank, they tend to buy bigger, more expensive houses, take luxury holidays several times a year, and own top-of-the-range cars. The larger the property, the higher the council tax, essential bills and maintenance costs. The more expensive the car, the higher the service charges. It can become a vicious circle, though there is nothing wrong with it, if people want to do it and can afford it. I'm a capitalist at heart and believe that if you work hard then you deserve all you achieve.

Quality and value are the most important things in terms of having a really enjoyable life. There is an excellent book called Essentialism by Greg McKeown that I would recommend. It's all about the pursuit of less: actively seeking out high quality but fewer things. In consciously choosing to do things wholeheartedly, or saying no to them altogether, we can focus on what is essential to us and to achieving our goals. As a result, we will be happier overall. It is the opposite of 'having it all' or feeling we 'have to do everything'.

This principle can be applied to all areas of people's lives. Once we have identified the things we truly value and enjoy, we can focus on those and do more of them by keeping within a budget. If eating good food is something we value highly, we might choose to cook more of our own gourmet meals rather than eating out, or shopping around for high-quality ingredients at lower prices or even growing our own vegetables. And then, once in a while, we can eat out at our favourite restaurant as a treat. The key is that we have identified good food as one of the things we truly value, and we can put other things we value less highly to one side.

The financial diet

With rising inflation and the associated increase in the cost of living, people can find their budgets are restricted. This is a good time to try one of my challenges: a one-month **financial diet.**

In a standard lifetime, most people learn more skills and increase their income through better-paid employment. They then spend more of that income in buying and maintaining a bigger house and a more extravagant lifestyle. But if they were to imagine for one month that they had only a third or a half of their actual salary, and they budgeted to live within that amount, most people find they could actually manage quite well. If we take the time to assess where and how we spend our money, we typically find that around 20% or 30% can be saved at any one point.

If this level of savings were kept up, the potential could be life changing. People could put the new savings to one side and, for example, retire early and do all the things they want to do. They could have all those experiences in the future that can really make life worth living.

This kind of exercise can have a profound impact on life

and how you view it. At one point, I retrained for a job and as a result I was living for a time on £1,000 a month, so I had to say no to lots of things. This turned out to be a powerful and useful thing to do because, in the process, I realised there were several things I didn't actually miss and it really highlighted the things that I valued the most and gave me most joy: my 20%.

I would encourage everyone to step off life's hamster wheel once in a while and take a bird's eye view of what matters in your life and what is actually non-essential – it offers a completely different perspective.

As people get older, they tend to fall into a pattern of behaviour that is familiar to them, but if they are willing to expand their horizons and experiment by trying different ways of reducing their spending, and this could have a very positive effect on their financial future. As well as reducing their current expenditure and increasing their potential savings, they might find they would be comfortable living off less money than they had previously thought in retirement and discover it could be possible for them to stop working earlier than planned.

Once a person has acquired a certain lifestyle, cutting things out can feel quite difficult. But there are swaps that can be done so it can work quite effectively. Being in control of your financial future is also incredibly empowering.

The Pension and Lifetime Savings Association **sets out**

retirement living standards that are split into **minimum, moderate** and **comfortable** living standards. A single person will need £12,800 a year to achieve the minimum living standards, and a couple will need £19,900. For a moderate lifestyle, it would be £23,300 for a single person and £34,000 for a couple. For what the association calls 'comfortable' living standard, a single person would need £37,300 and a couple £54,500.

For most people who have paid off their mortgage, the **moderate living standards are sufficient.** Having an income of between £25,000 and £30,000 a year in retirement would be perfectly comfortable for most couples. This is obviously subjective, and for some it would not be enough. But it is very important that people go through the process of working out how much money they feel they need in retirement in terms of their essential and discretionary spending. It may be less than they had thought.

People often think that they will need the same amount of income from their pension for every year of their retirement. In reality, they will probably be more active in the early phase of retirement and will spend more then than they will later. A graph of spending after retirement shows a curve going up and peaking, and then declining, usually after the age of 75, as people stop doing various things they used to spend money on, either from choice or for health reasons.

Spending a little bit less money earlier in life in order to retire sooner means we can enjoy a more active retirement for longer.

Shortcuts

- Our **likes and dislikes**, and what we find we **need and don't really need**, determine our lifestyles.

- **Essential spending** covers household bills – everything that is needed to run a home and you should review these regularly.

- **Discretionary spending** pays for our activities, hobbies and passions – the things that make us truly happy and so you want to make sure you can afford these for as long as possible.

- **80% of people's joy will come from 20% of their activities.** Invest in making your life more enjoyable and ask yourself the question; If I had all the time and all the money in the world, what would I do?

- Find **what truly makes you happy** and focus on the things that enhance your lifestyle, whatever your budget.

- We **value** things differently in the different **seasons** of our life. As we evolve, so too do our spending habits. Accept and embrace the changes and don't compare yourself with your younger identity.

- Living below your current means increases your future means. Trying the **financial diet** for just one month usually reveals 20% to 30% potential savings.

- Staying on the financial diet can be **life-changing,** allowing more money to be put aside.

- Working out how much you truly need for a **comfortable retirement** may allow you to **retire sooner** than you thought.

- Most people's **monthly expenditure reduces in later retirement** by around 1/3rd from age 75. Plan to spend more when younger and healthier in early retirement to account for this.

- Buy things that last and are worth the price.

- Don't just say, I'm terrible with money. You've learnt to walk, speak a language, drive and may even have become a parent. Leaning to budget, saving for a house, your family & your retirement isn't as hard and something you will always be better off being able to do.

Chapter 5: Families

Entering into a partnership with someone else, perhaps marrying or starting a family has a major impact on our financial situation and is often the catalyst for a new raft of decisions which hadn't been necessary before. Life was simple when you only had yourself to consider and now the dynamic shifts as compromise, sharing and responsibilities create different financial paths for us.

The high cost of weddings sometimes puts people off getting **married**, and more couples live together for longer before tying the knot, or they never make their partnership official in the eyes of the law. One reason fewer people are getting married may be the fear of divorce. 41% of marriages that took place in 1996 ended in divorce by the twenty-fifth anniversary and this tends to jump out to some people, those especially who are risk averse in relationships. However, this figure also means 59% of married couples were still going strong after their twenty-fifth anniversary, though that statistic rarely gets reported! There is also something of a downward trend in the divorce rate with more recent marriages, but the relatively high chance of divorce and the expense and emotional trauma that goes with it does make many people think twice about marriage.

Financially speaking, being part of a couple means you can **pool your incomes** and **share living costs**, creating a **higher**

disposable income. You can also borrow more as a couple and get a bigger **mortgage.** Going from an individual to a family unit in this way makes many things more possible.

There are tax advantages to being married or in a civil partnership: **any asset can be gifted between spouses, tax-free.** People who have investments or property can transfer ownership to their spouse without any tax consequences; this is especially relevant if one half of the couple is a non or basic-rate taxpayer while the other is a higher-rate taxpayer. Gifting large parts of buy-to-let properties, investment portfolios or savings, or even paying into partners' pensions if they have available allowances, effectively doubles their available tax allowances as a couple, ensuring that, as a unit, they keep more of their money.

Spouses are also not liable for **inheritance tax** (the same tax rules apply to civil partners). Even if someone marries their long-term partner on their deathbed, as many people have done, they will avoid paying inheritance tax.

A proportion of **income tax allowances** can also be shared. If the lower earner in a married couple or civil partnership earns less than the personal allowance (£12,570) or does not pay income tax at all, they can benefit from Marriage Allowance, which allows them to transfer £1,260 of their personal allowance to their spouse or civil partner (who must pay tax at the basic rate), reducing their overall tax bill as a couple. This is particularly useful for retirees and younger families.

There is a growing trend in developed economies of people deciding to have fewer children or not to not start a family, for a wide range of reasons. These can be financial or career-related and are sometimes principled, as when people decide that bringing another human being into the world would put an extra burden on our strained environment. Populations are already declining in most developed regions of the world and the global population is expected to peak in the second half of this millennium and then begin to decline. Typically, 18% of women in the UK will not have had children by the end of their childbearing years. This is unchanged from the 1950's but the major change in trends is that over 50% will now have their first child in their 30s. As people are living longer, they tend not to rush into the next phase of their lives as quickly as before, with many people savouring each decade as they go through them.

As individual choice has become more mainstream and accepted, there has been an increase in the number of childless couples, which in financial terms, are known as 'DINK'S' – **double income, no kids**. They are likely to have a higher cashflow and take frequent holidays and can continue this lifestyle throughout their thirties, forties and beyond. Many choose never to take the step back or pause from their careers associated with bringing up children and continue to pool resources with their partner, often in pursuit of lifestyle – or for some it's just never the right time.

DINK's can benefit by avoiding the need to pay a premium to live in the catchment area of a desirable school and by travelling outside of school holidays. Some of them will target an early retirement or a move to part-time work, while others might make their career the main focus of their lives. Some people just want to spend more quality time as a couple, enjoying life together.

Starting a family

For many people, deciding to start a family can come about for a whole myriad of reasons. Some plan meticulously and others have accidents; for some new parents it can really feel like it's somehow arrived out of nowhere! One day you were two and then the world changes overnight. There is no going back to how life was before and at this point, for many people, their purpose becomes clear. Financial decisions soon become more important as the family grows, and choices need to be made. There are more mouths to feed and bodies to clothe and a need for more space to grow into. Access to education, healthcare, housing and the need to insure this increased expenditure must all be considered.

The current figure attached to bringing up a child in the UK is **£10,000 per year.** Given that a growing number of children are staying with their parents until the age of 21, that could be a total of **£210,000** per child for the time they are living at home. This doesn't include the impact of the Bank of Mum and Dad, with parents giving an average gift of around **£20,000 as a deposit for a child's first home** (the average first-time buyer now buys at 33), helping with **wedding** expenses (the average first wedding now happens age 31), and making various other financial contributions where funds are available.

Starting a family triggers a range of additional expenses other than the need to clothe and feed another human being. You might need a **bigger car**, or a **bigger house**, possibly with a garden. Then there are **family holidays**, children's hobbies and activities, and the extra expense of birthdays and Christmas. All these things add up. They also need to be bought from our **taxed income.** Taking the figure of £10,000 per child per year, an extra annual income of £14,705 would be needed for basic rate taxpayers; £17,241 for higher rate taxpayers, and £18,867 for additional rate taxpayers. (A quick and handy way to work out the gross earnings required to deliver a sum net of tax and National Insurance is to divide the net figure by 0.68 for basic rate, 0.58 for the higher rate and at 0.53 for the additional rate taxpayers; this factors basic rate income tax at 20%, higher rate at 40%, additional rate at 45% plus National Insurance at 12%

for earnings at the basic tax rate and 2% for earnings above the higher rate threshold.)

Parents must either make these additional earnings or reduce their standard of living. Most people find themselves **spending less on themselves** and they forgo a lot of things: they don't eat out as much as they used to and they cut back on non-essentials and luxuries. Children are to some extent 'self-policing' in this respect, since going to an expensive restaurant is not a four-year old's idea of the ideal outing!

The cost of **childcare** in the UK can be quite high – more than people's mortgage payments in some areas. There is some government support. All three- and four-year-old children are eligible to 15 hours of free care and education a week for 38 weeks p.a. Most working families of three- and four-year-olds are eligible for 30 hours care for 38 weeks; the families must earn more than the equivalent of 16 hours per week on the minimum wage and both parents must earn less than the threshold of £100,000 p.a. (if one parent earns £100,001 p.a. the family will not be eligible, regardless of the other parent's income. Two parents earning £99,999 p.a. each would be eligible.)

If the childcare sums don't add up, perhaps because one parent's salary only barely covers the cost of childcare, many couples decide that the parent with the lower salary will take a **career break** instead. Traditionally it was always the mother who took **maternity leave**, and often an extended break when that ended. Two weeks paid **paternity leave** was introduced in the UK in 2003 and many employers offer more generous extensions of paternity leave. Nowadays, there has been a shift towards **shared parental leave** and there is a growing number of **stay-at-home dads**. Some new parents choose to **move nearer to their relatives** for family support and the benefit of free childcare.

Many people who stay at home to look after their children find they don't necessarily go back to their old jobs. They have found a new purpose in their lives and they don't want to give that up, especially in the children's early years when they want to spend time with them to make memories. However, during a **career break**, the ability to **save** and to pay into a **pension** reduces significantly, as does disposable income. These things do take their toll and there is a balance to be struck. Though there is more flexibility these days, it can sometimes be hard for parents who have taken a career break to get back into employment at the level they were before they had children. As children get older, of course, there is less incentive for parents to want to be at home because the children don't want to hang out as much with their parents anymore!

Parents who take a career break and stop paying their National Insurance contributions can automatically get **National Insurance credits** if they are claiming **child benefit** for their children under the age of 12. Since 6 April 2011 a specified adult, looking after a child under 12, can apply to be credited with Class 3 National Insurance contributions even if they don't qualify for the child benefit and haven't claimed it. These credits will count towards 'qualifying years' for their state pension. Anyone who registers with the Department for Work and Pensions can see their state pension service statement online and identify any gaps in their contributions.

If one parent earns more than £50,000, they must pay back 1% of their family's child benefit for every £100 they earn over £50,000. This means that anyone earning £60,000 and more will pay back 100% of their child benefit. This is called the **high-income child benefit charge**, and it is paid back in the form of income tax through self-assessment. This creates an anomalous situation, similar to the 'eligible working family' rule for free childcare, where two parents earning £49,999 each would be entitled to full child benefit, but if one parent earns £60,000 and the other only earns £10,000, they will lose all their child benefit. It is possible to **offset** all of your **pension contributions** against your '**adjusted net income**'. It is worth doing the sums to see if your pension contributions bring you down below the £50- £60,000 net figure and perhaps considering **increasing**

your pension contributions, which is in any case a highly tax-efficient way to save money.

Even if you end up repaying all of your child benefit through the high-income child benefit charge, it is still worth registering for the benefit so that you receive the national insurance credits mentioned above.

There is also an allowance for foster parents to cover the cost of bringing up a foster child. People who adopt a child, or children, can claim **statutory adoption pay and leave**. Their adopted children are entitled to the same child benefits as if they were the biological children of their parents.

Some couples, of course, struggle to conceive and end up spending significant sums on IVF. Most things have a financial cost, even this potentially life-changing procedure, and the money has to be found from disposable income.

If people looked at having children based purely on a financial calculation, we would possibly all decide to remain childless; it is not necessarily a rational thing to do. But most people with children would of course argue that the rewards are, quite literally, priceless. Parenthood also gives people a greater level of purpose and a structure to their lives as well as a higher perceived value on anything bought for their children's pleasure.

Education

One consideration for a lot of people is the type of education they want for their children. Should they commit to paying for a private education if they can afford to or should they consider moving to be in the catchment area of a particularly good state school? There are costs associated with both options. According to government figures, the **average price of a property** in the UK as of January 2023 was £290,000 and property close to a **state school rated 'outstanding'** by OFSTED would cost an average of **11% more**, meaning that parents would pay almost **£32,000 extra** on average for the privilege of their children going to that school. In areas of more expensive housing, of course, the real premium is considerably higher. Parents might then also choose to pay for extracurricular activities for their children to round off their education.

When the children have left school and there is no need to live in that same area, parents might choose to move to a cheaper property further away from the school and save the profit on the move.

Paying over the odds for a property in the catchment area of a good state school is still far cheaper than paying for **private education**. According to the Financial Times, the average fee for independent schools is currently **£15,191** per child per year. This increases to **£36,000** for children who **board** at a private school. This means that a higher rate taxpayer would need to earn £60,000 before tax to pay for the cost of one child boarding at a private school.

Many people who went to private school themselves choose to provide a similar education for their children. Private schools offer an excellent education with a wider range of choice of subjects and extracurricular activities. They provide access to a useful network of people in later life and can open doors to many different opportunities. It's a big commitment and a very personal choice. If parents do choose to send their children to a private school, they need to be sure they can cover the costs whatever happens. In my experience, most people would rather go without almost anything than take their children out of private education once they have started. Private school fees normally go up by a minimum of 5% each year and typically at more than the rate of inflation. It is wise to have **insurance** in place so that if personal circumstances change, the fees can continue to be paid and the children do not have to leave their school.

Sandwich generation

The **sandwich generation** is a name given to the generation of people who find themselves caring for both their aging parents and their own children: their children are typically staying at home for longer than before, while their parents are living longer than previous generations and are more likely to need some form of care.

One key factor encouraging children to stay longer at their parents' home is to save money for a deposit on their own house as they start to earn their own income but continue to live rent free with mum and dad. In 2021–2022, **the average age of first-time buyers** in the UK was **33.**

The Bank of Mum and Dad, as mentioned earlier, is likely to contribute to the deposits on their children's first house. This can be an effective way of reducing the parents' estate to reduce eventual inheritance tax liability while enjoying the benefit of seeing their children establish their own households. Parents are allowed to gift up to £3,000 per year to children tax free (this is the maximum annual amount, not the amount per child), so it can be wise to start making regular contributions to a savings fund before the children are ready to buy their first house.

Where children are moving into their first house with a new partner, parents are understandably worried that half of their gift towards the deposit on the house may end up benefiting the child's partner in the event of a breakup. It is possible to ringfence the contribution by setting up an agreement that the child who has been gifted the money owns a higher proportion of the property; if the parents contributed 5% of the value of the property, for example, it could be agreed that their child owns 55% of the equity in that property to their partner's 45%. This is a bit like a 'prenuptial' agreement and some people may find it uncomfortable, but it avoids the pain of writing a large cheque, only to see half of the benefit go to the now ex-partner if a breakup happens further down the line.

Although there is less expectation these days that children will look after their parents physically, many people in the sandwich generation do find themselves contributing in many ways to their aging parents' care. People who do not have children will need to rely on their own money to pay for care fees, and build their own network of people to look after them in old age. This is something they need to consider in their financial planning.

Divorce

Divorce has a lot of financial implications. The first is **maintenance payments for children** until they are financially independent, which is the later of when they become 21 or finish further education. The second is **maintenance for spouses** until they remarry, which can provide an incentive for the spouse not to remarry.

My advice for people when they get divorced is to complete the process as soon as possible, pay the price to have a clean split, and then move on. It is unlikely that the two of you will be getting on well at that point, and it is less painful for both parties to be able to resolve things quickly and get on with their new lives. If there are children, the divorcing couple should consciously make the process as amicable as possible to make things better for the children and to make continued access to the children by both parties easier.

The **matrimonial home** will typically go to whoever in the couple is looking after the children. The person who must leave the home may find it difficult to buy another property because they need to apply for a mortgage on their own and their level of borrowing is now restricted. If there is still a mortgage on the matrimonial home, the mortgage lender must also agree to a **single mortgage** for the person who continues to live there, and will assess affordability, and may decide that they can no longer afford to pay the mortgage on their single income. The only option in this case, difficult though it is, may be to sell the property and buy a smaller house with a more affordable mortgage. It is very hard, but divorce can lead to dreams crashing down.

Pensions are likely to be an important part of any divorce settlement as they can represent a high proportion of either partner's assets. There are usually three main options. One is to **offset** the value of a pension against some other aspect of the settlement, typically the property: Partner A keeps their pension, but partner B gets a bigger share of the property. My recommendation would be option two: **splitting** the pension by transferring a portion of it into the other partner's name. This leaves both parties in full control of what is now their pension. The third option is an **attachment** or **earmarking** order, where it is agreed that one partner will get a portion of the benefits of a pension when the partner who keeps the pension starts to draw it. This means that the partner for whom part of the pension is 'earmarked' has to wait until the other partner decides to draw their pension before they can receive any pension themselves. This may be the only option for some final salary pensions.

Another reason to favour splitting a pension and giving away a portion of it is that pensions can be built up again quite quickly, thanks to tax relief.

Having a **clean exit** is by far and away the most successful way of finalising a divorce. The older people are when they get divorced, the harder it can be because they have got used to a certain standard of living, a particular size of house, and a certain quality of holiday etc. After a divorce, people can only usually afford maybe half of what they had before, and it can be more difficult to build their finances up again. They become dependent on their health and their ability to carry on working for longer. A lot of people stay together for the sake of their children and divorce later, when the children are older. But if a marriage is not working, the sooner a couple can split, the better able they are to move on. There is then also a greater chance that both parties will find someone else to have a happy life with.

When thinking about starting a family, it is a very good idea to **plan ahead**, consider the likely costs and budget appropriately for them. It is also a very good idea to carry out a **stress test** and consider what pressure you would be under financially if your circumstances changed. As we discuss in a later chapter, **insurance** can be a great reassurance. As soon as a couple starts a family, their attitude to insurance changes completely. They need to consider the impact that a serious accident or the death of one, or both parents might have on their children. This alters people's perceptions of life and their priorities and is a major catalyst towards a change of mindset.

I have talked to couples who were planning for children but unexpectedly ended up with twins, or even triplets. This can be of course incredibly joyful but also difficult to plan for and a lot of help and support is needed. People in this situation should go back to the drawing board to work out what they need to do. Their life has changed, unexpectedly and forever. It can be challenging but it certainly won't be dull!

I would strongly recommend that people in married couples or civil partnerships look at their finances and assets on a **joint basis.** If you use a financial adviser, **attend meetings together** so that one half of the couple is not making all the financial decisions by themselves. If both people in the couple are involved, the greater the success of their financial planning and the more chance that they can make most effective use of their separate allowances etc. It is unfortunately very common for one partner to be more active in financial matters and for the other to 'take a back seat.' But if one of them dies unexpectedly or has a serious accident that affects their decision-making, there is an added layer of stress if the remaining partner is in the dark about their finances.

Having a family gives people an anchor which leads to stronger financial plans, a greater conviction about what they are going to do, and a clearer idea of how they want to pass things on. They are more concerned with planning financial structures and their goals become clearer. There can be a greater clarity of purpose that comes with marriage and having children than if someone is on their own.

When a couple's children start families of their own, this creates a new and exciting series of 'firsts' with the grandchildren: the first smile, the first step, the first words... This experience can provide an injection of energy and joy in later life.

Life is a lottery. We never really know which way it is going to go when there are many swings and roundabouts. But that's the fun of it!

Shortcuts

- Being married is really tax efficient as **any asset can be gifted** between spouses free of tax; a proportion of **tax allowances** can also be passed to spouses to reduce tax liabilities. There is no **inheritance tax** on money and assets passed on to a spouse on death.

- Couples **share living costs** and **pool incomes**, increasing their disposable income.

- Couples should review their finances and assets on a **joint basis** to make the most of their tax allowances and ensure **both parties are aware** of key financial arrangements.

- It costs around **£10,000 per child per year** to bring up children: **£210,000** over a typical 21 years of children living at home. Consider what savings you can make to absorb these costs more easily.

- **Childcare** is a major expense; more parents are choosing to take **career breaks** to look after children and living near **grandparents** can offer respite from these costs.

- **Properties** in the catchment areas of good **state schools** cost an average **11% more.** Consider renting for 6 months in this area to get the initial place. If you buy, the value is usually well insulated form market movements.

- People are reluctant to take children out of **private education** once they have started; it is wise to consider **insurance** against changing circumstances.

- Teach children about money early. The sooner they understand it the greater they value it and feel comfortable planning with it later in life.

- **Pensions** are an increasingly important part of **divorce** settlements and are better shared if you have the career time left to rebuild the pot. It builds faster due to the extra tax relief on contributions, especially for higher and additional rate tax payers.

- A **clean exit** is the most successful way of finalising a divorce; it may be necessary to **downsize** houses if mortgages become unaffordable for individuals after the split.

- The **sandwich generation** can find themselves simultaneously caring for elderly parents and their own children. Plan ahead for this as much as possible, consider what may be your priority and how you can adapt over time.

Chapter 6: Property Planning

They say an Englishman's home is his castle and **home ownership** is a goal of most people. The 2021 UK census shows that 62.5% of UK households own the accommodation they live in, and that 33% of households are mortgage free and own their homes outright.[4]

There is still a general shortage of housing in the UK. The government has a target of building 300,000 homes per year by the mid-2020s, but in 2021 only 157,000 new homes were built in the UK against a target of 180,000, according to a House of Commons Committee Report.[5] During the years of Margaret Thatcher's premiership, people who had rented council properties for more than three years were given the right to buy them at a discount. The maximum discount was 60% on houses after 30 years' tenancy, and 70% on flats after 15 years. Although this had the desired effect of increasing homeownership, it also depleted the UK's stock of social housing, a shortfall that has still not been made good. These factors contribute to the high price of housing in the UK.

Most people like to own property. They like to own the roof over their heads, it makes them feel secure and wealthy: their houses reflect their **earnings and success**. Property is easy for people to understand and all homeowners quickly become quite expert in the local housing market. It isn't possible to

[4] Housing, England and Wales - Office for National Statistics (ons.gov.uk)

[5] The Affordable Homes Programme since 2015 - Committee of Public Accounts (parliament.uk)

generalise about the market geographically. Property prices are generally highest in London and the southeast of the country, but in every part of the UK, people see value in different things. House-hunters looking for a property in a city, in a suburb or in the commuter belt all have different requirements, whether that is in Manchester, Leeds or London. There are even variations within areas of individual cities, with London's boroughs being a good example. All of these things get factored into the price of properties around the country.

Property is not an exact science, and the more specialised knowledge someone has of an area, the more efficiently they can buy property. One important thing to remember is that **buying a house to live in** is a very different scenario to buying property as an **investment purchase**, and vice versa.

The cost of **maintenance** is something everyone should consider before buying a property. Every house will need redecorating regularly: windows and flooring deteriorate; the roof will need attention sooner or later; electrics and plumbing need to be upgraded every 10 to 15 years. Fashions for fixtures and fittings come and go, and old ones come to look incredibly dated – people will probably want new furniture, a new kitchen and a new bathroom perhaps every 15 to 20 years. All these things represent an ongoing cost to the homeowner. Accidents and freak weather occurrences can also happen though, happily, rarely: fires or gas explosions, lightning strikes or freak floods. These risks will be covered by household insurance – though floods are becoming more common as we experience more frequent heavy and prolonged rainfall and properties that are now regularly prone to flooding may struggle to insure the risk.

The house-buying season

The house-buying season unofficially starts at the Easter weekend, which coincides with school holidays and the arrival of spring. Flowers are blooming, leaves are coming into bud, and there may even be some sunshine after the long grey UK winter, so people are more open to moving during this period. There is optimism all around and people start thinking about their dream house and the life that will go with it. The market gets busier and busier throughout the summer, and house prices reflect this growing demand. At a time when lots of people want to buy, vendors will typically get higher prices. Property 'chains', where the sale of one property is dependent on the sale of the buyer's own property, and so on up and down the line, are less problematical because properties are changing hands more quickly.

The market tails off in October because most people do not want to move in the winter. It also typically takes three months from putting a house on the market to completion of the sale, so putting a house on the market in October would mean moving at Christmas. This is not usually a popular choice.

However, there are three main reasons why people will want to sell or move house regardless of the time of year: death, birth and divorce. Someone who has inherited a house may want to sell it to distribute money to the beneficiaries of the previous owner's will; a family having a baby may need more space; a couple going through a divorce may need to sell and divide the proceeds. All these scenarios also mean that a quick sale is preferable and anyone looking to buy out of season from this kind of buyer can normally negotiate better prices.

In property, there are **buoyant and downward seasons**, just as there are in most markets. When there is high employment and interest rates are low, people feel positive about the future and borrowing is relatively cheap. Even though property prices will be rising at these times, this doesn't deter people because they believe prices will continue to rise, and they fear 'missing out' if they don't buy sooner rather than later.

When interest rates rise, unemployment starts to increase and there may be a recessionary period, people are less optimistic and find it more difficult to get easy, low-cost credit. They are more likely to try to negotiate prices down and will probably carry out more due diligence before making any offers. More sales fall through before completion and prices fall. Both these effects are often exacerbated by estate agents who will talk up prices in a rising market and push for quick sales at lower prices in falling markets.

There are also certain fads and trends in property, such as the trend for buying more spacious houses in the country which was prevalent during the COVID-19 pandemic. People were increasingly working from home, living in the country offered a more pleasant environment to live in, and they didn't expect to have to commute to the office so often in the future, if at all. With the gradual return to office work, this trend reversed as people found there is more commuting involved than they had imagined, life is generally less convenient in terms of local shops and facilities and perhaps they can't get into a good school because catchment areas are smaller in the country. With the rise in energy prices, people are becoming more conscious of how well houses are insulated, which tends to favour newer houses. There are times when flats or bungalows are more in vogue. All of these trends affect market prices.

In November 2022, the **average house price in the UK** rose to **£295,000**. That was 10% higher than the year before, largely because in the lead up to Brexit there was uncertainty about how house prices would be affected, and many people waited to see what would happen before putting their property in the market. This created a lot of pent-up demand and an eventual surge in prices.

For that average house price, a buyer would need roughly **£15,000** for a 5% deposit, while **£30,000** would be required for a 10% deposit. The average salary, net of tax, is between £26,000 and £27,000, so a deposit represents perhaps **two years'** worth of net savings. This is not easy for many young people, which is where the ever-popular **Bank of Mum and Dad** often steps in to help.

Buying a home

In the house-buying process, there are two sides to the equation: the **vendor** selling the property, who usually wants the highest offer, and the **buyer** who wants to feel they have got the best possible price.

It is well worth buyers doing their research before putting in an offer on a property. They should view as many properties as possible in the same area, even if they are not exactly what they think they are looking for. This helps them to see the space and location they can afford for their budget and gives them a better view of the kind of property they want. Rightmove and Zoopla are useful tools because they list prices of **recently sold properties** in the same area or street. **Neighbourhood websites** can be useful sources of information about local issues such future housing developments, flood risks and crime statistics. Buyers should also get quotes for any improvement work required to make the property a liveable space, so they have a good idea of the total amount of money they need.

Buyers should always ask the estate agent why the vendor is selling. Perhaps they are downsizing, or maybe they have inherited the house. This can help the buyer understand whether the vendor wants a quick sale so a deal might be reached, or they can afford to wait for the best offer. It may also reveal that buyer is unhappy with the property and wants to leave, in which case it worth finding out why.

If a buyer is in a chain themselves, they will probably have to pay a slightly higher purchase price because they cannot guarantee a swift turnaround and chains can break down. If anyone involved in the chain needs to put their property back on the market because their sale has fallen through, there can be a delay of several months. The vendor wants to sell their property as quickly and as painlessly as possible, so a 'cash buyer' can often get the best price - someone who has already sold their own property and has the money for the deposit in the bank and a mortgage already agreed, or who can afford to buy the property outright without a mortgage. First-time buyers are also favoured, because they are also 'chain free' and will typically have their mortgage agreed in principle. In times of high demand, buyers will need to show that they have an agreed sale for their own house and that there are no uncertainties further down the chain. Estate agents tend to describe buyers who cannot be certain they will quickly sell their own property as 'non-proceedable.' Finding a house that you like and putting in an offer before you have even put your own house on the market is a rare occurrence.

The average time for a house purchase from **offer to completion** is **three months.** Once an offer is accepted on a property and the mortgage offer is confirmed, a survey is carried out to confirm that there are no structural problems or concerns about potential subsidence, and that the electric and plumbing are in good working order etc.. Solicitors must then run searches, check compliance and run due diligence, checking land boundaries, obtaining proof that home improvements have been certified by building regulations officers and that any necessary planning permission was given and so on. All of this takes time. The process can drag on if there are queries that need to be resolved and the vendors can't find the evidence.

One useful tip: even if a buyer really loves a property, they should never say so to the vendor or their agent! They should point out things they don't like about it or that need improvement. If the estate agent knows how much a buyer likes a property, they will encourage their vendor to reject an early offer and try to create a bidding war between buyers.

Indemnity insurance can be useful to speed up the buying process. If there are any issues that can't be resolved, such as the vendor being unable to provide a building regulations certificate for improvements that have been carried out, or uncertainties about whether something contravenes a restrictive covenant that may apply to the property, the vendor can take out insurance to indemnify the buyer against all of their costs, including legal costs. Such insurance is normally relatively inexpensive, because the risk of there being a serious problem is very low. Buyers can then proceed knowing that if there is a problem after they buy a property, all their costs incurred will be covered by the insurance.

When vendors have lived in their home for many years, they tend to have a **disproportionate view of its value.** They will often believe that any money they have spent on the property will have added to its value, but this is not always the case. Buyers may not like the style of a kitchen or bathroom, for example, even though it may have been replaced quite recently. It all comes down to personal taste. Vendors should be careful not to spend too much on **improvements to a property** they intend to sell in the hope that this will increase the value. The more expensive a property is then the more likely this will be true, as their owners tend to be able to afford very personal tastes in decor and design. A buyer may be happy to accept that, for example, the wiring in a property will need replacing, or that they need to instal new double glazing. Vendors can be better off offering a discount on the asking price to take account of the work needed rather than paying to have the work done themselves. Relatively small amounts of money spent on redecorating, however, are nearly always money well spent, as is effort spent on decluttering. A freshly painted house with clear work surfaces and everything stored neatly away looks more appealing to buyers. It may be worth considering putting some furniture into storage while the house is on the market to make the house look bigger.

Selling a house with all its memories can also be very emotive for vendors. Sometimes they prefer to sell to a young couple just starting out or to a family, instead of a landlord, so it can be worthwhile for buyers to mention their particular story alongside a strong offer.

When buying or selling a house, once **contracts have been exchanged** the buyer and the vendor are legally committed to the deal and it is possible to sue someone who pulls out after this stage. Buyers are normally required to pay a deposit of 10%

on exchange, though 5% may be accepted where this is the most the buyer has been able to raise. Vendors can sue to keep the deposit if a buyer subsequently pulls out of a sale. If a lower deposit was agreed, they may still be able to sue for the full 10% and for additional compensation to cover any costs.

Buyers should keep some money in reserve for home improvements. It can be a good idea to live in a property for three to six months, before deciding what really needs to be changed. It is also possible to save substantial amounts of money by waiting for the summer or Black Friday sales, rather than rushing out and buying everything new the moment you move in – tempting though that often is!

Building wealth

Typically, **house prices** in the UK go up by an average of around 4-5% each year, meaning they generally double in value every 15 years. If a house is someone's main residence, any profit they make on it is completely tax-free. People can renovate and add value to properties, especially if they do a lot of the work themselves. They can learn how to strip things out, tear things down and build walls – all from YouTube videos!

People now own a proportion of their property, even though they still need to repay their mortgage, and as the value of their property increases and they pay down their mortgage, they are creating wealth. When prices are rising strongly, people can realise double digit returns. If someone gets a mortgage on a £500,000 property with a £50,000 deposit, and the value quickly increases by 10%, they have gained £50,000 and doubled their deposit: a good return on their investment!

Even though we normally look at 4% or even 5% increase in property prices averaged out over the long term, people can of course flip properties and do various things to achieve even better returns. With the right **knowledge of the local market** and perhaps skills in doing up properties ready for resale, they can outsmart the market and make higher returns.

Owning your own home can also be used to generate income: a furnished spare room in your main residence can be rented out and the first £7,500 a year of earnings from this rental is tax-free.

There is a certain level of **stability** within UK house prices and only a limited level of downside, partly because people do not tend to pay as much attention to the fluctuation of property prices as they do with stock market values. The **illiquidity of property** can sometimes be a benefit and at other times a pitfall. Stock markets respond rapidly because they are very liquid and very efficient at pricing in new information. Property, on the other hand, is very illiquid – it takes a long time to sell your asset and make a new investment – and the market is subject to a great deal of subjectivity. People who fall in love with a property will pay whatever they can afford to secure it. Certain locations carry a premium, as do older character properties. This illiquidity is quite useful when markets are dropping, and people are panicking because it gives them time to adjust to the new reality before they actually sell their home. Buyers have the opportunity to pull out of a house sale at any time before the exchange of contracts if they have a change of heart, whereas stocks can be sold in a moment of panic. When prices start to fall, people who do not need to sell their property or move house often decide to stay put and wait for an improvement in prices. In rising markets, however, they will normally notice if somebody in their street puts their house up for sale and they realise their house may be worth £100,000 more than they thought, in which case they may be tempted to put it on the market and move on. These two effects tend to dampen the effect of falls in the market but encourage the effect of rising markets: the overall effect is steadily rising house prices in the long term.

The property cycle

Homes offer different things to different people at different times of their life. A young person will typically be happy with a one-bed flat in **the right location** – they like an area with lots of activities and human interaction, perhaps near their place of work, and they are content with less space.

Couples with a young family need more space, usually in a house with stairs and a garden, in the suburbs, preferably close to good schools. The desire to replicate the homes we lived in when we were young is a common theme. This age group is also usually happy to **renovate** properties to add value to them so they can move up the property ladder.

Middle-aged parents might choose to **downsize** after their children have left home. They might choose to move to a flat closer to the centre of town, having enjoyed that lifestyle when they were younger. This can be particularly true when a couple is close to retiring and their neighbours also start to move on.

When people are less mobile in older age, they need a **property without much maintenance**, often preferably **without stairs**. Bungalows are very popular, but a premium is usually paid for them. There are also retirement villages or apartments that cater well for this phase in life.

The **housing ladder** is called that because the bottom rung is the lowest. People buy their first property, then they build up some equity or adjust their mortgage. They then have a bigger deposit and a new mortgage to buy a larger property – the next rung on the ladder – and so on. As they get older, they earn more and most people will buy a larger house when they can afford it. This is the typical arc that people go through with property. Once they reach retirement age, they can downsize and release some equity, either to fund their retirement tax-free, or to put into an annuity or investment.

The important thing to remember is that **no one property does it all.** We tend to look for the perfect place, our forever home, but it almost certainly doesn't exist. It's all about what best suits our needs at different times of life and what we are willing to compromise on: location, size, outside space, facilities and transport etc. The property that was perfect for us in our thirties may be less convenient in our fifties, and we must be willing to accept that. Any property someone buys probably has a 10-year horizon before they need to move on.

Some people want large houses, others don't – it's a very personal choice. When upsizing to a bigger property, it's important to factor in the cost of extra furniture, heating, insurance, maintenance and gardening, as well as the higher mortgage payments that typically go with it. But if a family needs more space, it is normally worth buying something at the top end of the budget rather than skimping on a place that is quickly outgrown as possessions accumulate and growing children want more space. A larger house will significantly improve the quality of life for that family for many years to come.

However, in other circumstances, it might not make financial sense to continue to pay for an extra bedroom or two that are used only occasionally. Many people keep larger houses than they need so that friends and family can stay perhaps only a few times per year. This is a very expensive thing to do, especially in cities. People may end up working 5 or 10 more years to pay off the mortgage for a larger house they do not really need. It could be far cheaper for them to pay for a hotel for their friends and relatives when they come to visit.

People like to feel that they have room to accommodate guests, but downsizing to a slightly smaller house or moving to less expensive area when there is no burning need to be in a particular location can allow people to pay off their mortgage sooner and retire earlier. People should ask themselves on a regular basis what the true value of a larger house is to them, and whether they really need the extra space. If the answer is yes, they should stick with it; if the answer is no, they should consider their options. People often say to me, 'Oh, but my brother wouldn't be happy for me to pay for a hotel for him and his family when they come to stay,' and I suggest they point out that they are funding perhaps an additional £100,000 of mortgage borrowing every year so that the family can stay occasionally in what is otherwise an empty bedroom, so they should be happy to accept an occasional free hotel stay instead!

Second properties

For many people the dream is to live in a house they love for 80% of the time and then to have a second property for the remaining 20%, perhaps somewhere peaceful in the **countryside** or a holiday home **overseas.**

There are many things to consider, including the extra expense and fuss of maintaining a **second property,** especially one outside the UK. There will be double the costs in terms of bills and people will not get the best value for money if they are only visiting three or four times a year. If someone buys overseas, they will typically pay 10% in **fees.** In countries such as France or Spain **deposits** of 15% or 20% for second home mortgages can be acceptable; mortgages in other countries might need as much as 30% or 40% deposit. **Stamp duty** on purchase of holiday properties is another important consideration, especially for second homes. Then there is likely to be an **additional 3% stamp duty** to pay on second homes in the UK as well as council tax. These taxes mount up.

Someone might decide to buy a holiday home in the UK, perhaps a bolthole in the country or by the sea where they can stay at weekends. It is very important to consider the impact of the journey to and from these holiday homes. If it is, let's say, a two-hour drive from where you live to the holiday home, how often will you feel like doing that on a Friday evening or a

Saturday morning after a busy week? How will you feel about the drive home after a weekend away? How tired will you feel on Monday morning when it's time to go to work again?

I hate to be a killjoy, but many people who buy a holiday home sell it sometime later when they find they are not spending enough time there to make it cost-effective.

There is also **upkeep** to consider. The upkeep of a holiday home could be as much as £1,000 a month when you consider council tax; the cost of keeping freezers running and perhaps some heating in the winter; ongoing maintenance and gardening costs etc. That equates to £12,000 a year. For that amount of money, you could rent someone else's property, possibly in a more desirable location, without the worry of being responsible for it the rest of the year. Or you could stay in a 5-star hotel. A holiday home ties people to a particular place, and they need to be certain they are happy to go there time after time, as opposed to being free to choose their destination.

That said, many people get great pleasure from knowing they have their own place in a location they love and feel attached to.

Holiday homes can also be rented out when they are not being used. This works for those with the time to devote to it, in terms of communicating with people who want to book and managing their stay, but for others it can be a hassle. A second property that is rented out as a **furnished holiday let** is a bit of a special case in tax terms, because it is treated as a trading business. The property must be let commercially for at least 105 days in the tax year. All mortgage interest payments can be set against profits, whereas interest relief on buy-to-lets is now restricted to a tax-credit for only 20% of mortgage interest payments. Capital expenditures on improvements, fixtures and fittings can also be set against profits, whereas only repairs, replacement furnishings or appliances are eligible for relief for a buy-to-let. Capital gains tax reliefs are available on the sale of a furnished holiday let and the property is exempt from inheritance tax because it is seen as a business. Finally, earnings from a furnished holiday let are 'pensionable' so tax relief can be claimed on any pension contributions made from the income.

It is important to remember the challenges of running a holiday let if your main residence is not nearby: beds need changing; rooms need cleaning; things need fixing; a garden needs to be taken care of. You need people you can rely on to do these things for you if you cannot get there to do them yourself.

A second property can of course be **rented out** on a permanent basis, but being a landlord is not for everyone. It works well for those who can be non-emotive and look at it purely as a business transaction. The types of properties offering the highest yields are not always the ones people dream about owning! There are lots of points to consider with buy-to-lets: rent increases in line with inflation should be passed on every year to tenants; there are void periods to take into account; and the rental income must be declared because it is taxable. Finding good long-term tenants is very important, and it is often worth looking at local council initiatives that guarantee to pay the rent even in void periods, and to cover for any damage by tenants, in order to attract private landlords to an area that is undersupplied with rental properties. Many people who do not like the management side of buy-to-let's use letting agents, with varying degrees of success. Agents will typically take one month's rent a year in fees, representing around 8% of rental income. Many landlords will now consider setting up a limited business to invest in property. This approach has both upsides and downsides which could fill a book in themselves, but the main things to consider whether to do this or not are centred around taxation. It's worth seeking specialist advice before proceeding.

When you come to sell a second property, remember only gains from the sale of one's main residence are tax-free, and profits may be liable to **capital gains tax**. If the property has been rented out for a proportion of the total period of ownership, gains are partially taxable, though there is **Private Residence Relief** for the period for which you lived in the property and an additional relief for **the last nine months of ownership**, even if you were not living in the property at the time.

Many people use an inheritance to buy a second property, but I often suggest considering **investing a lump sum** instead if you want simplicity and low maintenance. One could draw down perhaps 4% or 5% per annum on a sound investment without affecting the capital, as we were discussing earlier (the 'safe as houses' figure of 3.1% was a figure calculated across the last 100 years and every conceivable financial crisis) On a £100,000 lump sum, that would be £4,000 or £5,000 a year that could be used to rent somewhere anywhere in the world for holidays, or for a longer period. Drawing out dividends or income from investment is a useful investment strategy, and it can be tax-free if kept within ISAs, all without the time and trouble involved in owning a second property.

People who do own several properties, especially those who have reached retirement age, should regularly **reassess their property portfolios.** If they have several properties, they might decide to keep two because they are still good properties and they would buy them again if they could, and they could sell the others to simplify things and do something more enjoyable with the proceeds. When they sell and pay tax on those properties, on paper they will be poorer, but their wealth will be more liquid, and they will have more time and opportunity to spend their money.

Shortcuts

- The UK housing market is most active between **Easter** and **October** and so is the easiest time to buy and sell.
- **Births, deaths and divorces** are the main reasons for sales 'out of season' and can lead to lower negotiated prices.
- The housing market is stronger in times of **higher employment** and **lower interest rates.**
- The relative illiquidity of UK housing makes it a more **stable** market.
- Buying a house to **live in** and buying a house as an **investment** should be judged by very **different criteria.**
- Don't wait too long to get onto the ladder. Paying **rent is dead money** but paying a mortgage is a saving vehicle for the next step of the ladder.
- Always **research** an area well before buying a property. Try staying there for long weekends, try the commute and lifestyle facilities.
- Cash buyers and first-time buyers who are not involved in a **buying chain** will be able to negotiate the best prices for speed of completion and a low-stress process.

- Once contracts have been **exchanged**, you are **legally obliged** to go through with a sale and can be sued by the vendor for your deposit and any costs incurred if you pull out.

- Always keep 5% of the purchase price in reserve for **improvements**; it is a good idea to wait six months to see which are most important and to buy new furnishings, appliances etc. in sales where possible.

- Owning housing helps **build wealth**, and can **generate income** from rental.

- Different houses suit our needs best at **different stages of our lives**; asking ourselves if we would still buy the same house today can be an interesting exercise.

- Avoid a house that **stretches your finances to the maximum.** Keeping rooms available in houses that are **larger than we need** for occasional guests can be very expensive; consider **downsizing** and putting friends and family up in local hotels or guest houses when they visit.

- When buying a second property as a **holiday home**, think carefully about **journey times, upkeep** costs and the practicalities of **maintenance**; staying in hotels or renting holiday properties can be less expensive and more flexible.

- An **overseas holiday home** involves **further expense** and **greater difficulties** regarding maintenance but can offer a unique life experience. They are easy to buy but often difficult to sell so ensure this is affordable and a matches your longer-term aspirations.

- **Additional UK stamp duty** is payable on second homes but is refundable within 36 months if you sell your old main residence during that period.

- Holiday homes can be let out as **furnished holiday lets** with several tax advantages.

- If you own several rental properties, **reassess your portfolio** regularly and keep those that make life easier for you and sell those that make your life more difficult.

- **No property does everything** for you so betting the house on the house often falls short of expectations.

- **Don't borrow into retirement.** Health can fail unexpectedly, and the property can be lost. Often by the time you can enjoy it then it's time to downsize.

Chapter 7: Insurance

No one can predict what will happen in life. It's full of odd dangers, and that's why we tend to like safety nets. There is a whole industry dedicated to easing our worries around loss and risk and they supply us with insurance to offset these risks. Insurance can provide peace of mind that we are covered against the worst eventualities. Other than insuring their belongings, people tend to insure their financial future against three main risks: early death; serious illness and being unable to continue working. These are the main areas that I will cover in this chapter. I will let you know now that some of these things may seem a bit dry to read through, but they are actually really important to know, and I've tried my best to simplify everything as much as I can. I'd say this is the number one topic that people wish they had spent more time learning about when things go wrong in life, and I think I've managed to provide 99% of what you need to know in this chapter. Essentially, my view is that you can't build strong foundations on sand and if you want to build a strong and stable life then insuring against the worst gives you that solid foundation for you and your family's future.

Different types of personal insurance become more relevant at different stages in life. Up to and including the age of 18, children are typically the responsibility of their parents or guardians. Beyond this, we are financially independent and income protection cover may become useful as a safety net if you can't work for any reason. From 25-30 onwards, life insurance and critical illness cover is increasingly important as we become couples and family units. When we are young, of course, we tend to think that nothing bad will ever happen to us. As we get older, we begin to acknowledge that there is statistically more chance of developing a critical illness and of experiencing more of what life can throw at us, because something eventually does happen to us or to somebody we know. Because of this increasing risk, anyone who first insures themselves in their fifties and sixties will notice that premiums are much more expensive. It pays to plan ahead and take out the relevant insurance sooner rather than later.

As a general rule of thumb, every time someone experiences a major life event, they should review their protection. These events include moving house, a promotion, getting married or divorced, having a child and developing a serious illness. Arranging insurance through a broker means there will be regular reviews to look at the 'protection gap'. This will take into account things like changing income, expenditure and lifestyle, and what is required from insurance policies as a result. This process always includes some uncomfortable conversations about life-changing situations and playing the 'what if' game. If you and your partner have children, who would look after the children if one of you dies? Would parents or in-laws be able to help? What if someone needed care at some point? Could family members look after them or would you need to pay for that care?

Insurance allows us to take control of the 'what if' moments and reassures us that our foundations are solid. When life gets tough and the worst happens, we know we have insurance in place so that we and the people we care about the most will be able to manage in any eventuality.

Getting married or having children are often the biggest catalysts for people to start taking out personal insurance, because they realise that there is now someone very precious who depends on them and their being able to provide for them. They suddenly see vulnerabilities all around them and it changes their perspective on life. The vital question is always whether anyone has sufficient cover. A financial adviser can help work out how much cover is needed. The figure is different for everyone because we all have individual circumstances. If there was a product that would pay a tax free lump sum of maybe several hundred thousand pounds or even a million pounds to your family on death and the same if you had a critical illness, and that paid your current net salary if you couldn't work until retirement age – and it was free – then everyone would sign up to it. Nobody ever refuses death in service or sick pay at work, do they? The reality of course is that insurance isn't free. This is where it becomes important to really review your exposure to risk; how much you are willing to pay to acquire security and peace of mind; and then take action to put this into place. My hope is that you never have to claim on any policy but if you do, then it certainly helps reduce some of the impact from life's biggest curveballs.

> **Consider:** *first what your needs are and what the risks are that you're exposed to; secondly what budget you have available; and then finally maximise the cover to your most important needs.*

Life Cover

Life insurance pays out a tax-free lump sum if you die during the term of the policy, giving beneficiaries the flexibility to choose what to do with the money. It could be used to pay off a mortgage; to meet other capital liabilities such as a loan; to replace lost income; to pay for school and university fees; or to cover any outgoings your dependants would otherwise find it difficult to meet without your salary. The money could be invested and a regular income could be drawn from it. It could also be used to pay for a carer to look after someone when you are no longer around to help.

Before taking out a life insurance policy, check whether you are entitled to death in service cover through your employment.

Critical illness cover and income protection cover may also be included. These are known as a P11D benefits which means no tax is payable on them, so they are doubly advantageous: the premiums are covered by your employer and you don't have to pay them from your taxed income. **Death in service** cover is usually calculated at between three- and five-times annual salary. This might not be sufficient for your needs, in which case you might also consider taking out a supplementary policy of your own. Make sure you know what you may be entitled to as part of your employment package before taking any further steps. Bear in mind that you will lose this cover if you move to a different employer and the new employer may not match the same level of cover, in which case, again, you should consider taking out an additional policy.

Start young. The younger someone is when they take out a personal insurance policy, the cheaper the premiums. Starting a life insurance policy in your twenties or thirties may not seem like a high priority, but it is an effective way of protecting yourself in the long run. You can enhance or increase your cover later in life when you are more likely to have dependants who rely on you financially and when they are grown up and you have built up more financial assets then you can reduce or cancel your cover when it's no longer needed. The typical time to enhance a policy is on marriage or entering into a partnership, or after starting a family. It is often **cheaper to amend an**

existing policy than to take out a new one, which is why it pays to start early.

It is very important that people disclose their **full medical history** when applying for life insurance as this will reduce the chances of an eventual claim being rejected. Anyone with a pre-existing condition can still find suitable life insurance, but it may be more expensive. Although the plan may be loaded on the premium, it's important to remember that there is a more likely chance of this being paid out due to health conditions and if you have been honest at the application stage then you know it will pay out in the event of a claim.

With life insurance, 98% of all claims are paid out because it is a fairly straightforward policy; proof of death in the form of a death certificate is usually all that is required. The main reason a claim might be rejected is if medical records reveal that someone has died from a condition they did not disclose or, for example, if they were a smoker, but they had applied as a non-smoker.

The payout is **not subject to income tax** if the policy is classified as a **qualifying** policy. Different rules apply to **non-qualifying** policies which are effectively those with a form of investment that will build a value at the end of the policy. Generally, all standard term policies will be qualifying and tax free. However, any lump sum may become liable for **inheritance**

tax (IHT) if it is part of someone's estate, and the value of the estate, including the life insurance payout, exceeds the nil rate band per person, which is set at £325,000 for 2023-24. This does not apply when the lump sum goes directly to a spouse or civil partner. If a life insurance policy is put in trust, the beneficiaries will not have to pay IHT on the payout. Life insurance trusts are generally very simple and free to set up at the time of application. They ensure the payout is swift and the proceeds go to whomever you want to benefit. In order to understand the implications of putting a life insurance policy in trust, it is wise to talk to an expert financial adviser.

The ideal amount of cover to take out on a life insurance policy will depend on individual circumstances and the cost of the premiums. The number of dependants someone has will often determine the level of cover, since every child represents an extra cost. A figure of 10 times a person's annual income is sometimes suggested as the ideal; most people find that cover of £500,000 suits their needs. The higher the amount of cover, the more expensive the premiums.

People usually include an amount for funeral expenses and for paying off an existing mortgage or other debts. If they have children, they should consider how much money would be needed to cover childcare costs and school or university fees and expenses, up to the point where they finish their education and start out in the world of work. These days, children are not usually self-sufficient and independent until about the age of 23, so that should be factored in. If a parent were to die, they would probably also want to provide some sort of legacy for each of their children, perhaps a deposit for a house.

> **Consider:** *could you or your surviving spouse or partner afford the mortgage payments on their own in the event of death? Would all your children's needs be financially funded if one of you wasn't there supporting the family with an income or assisting with child support?*

There are two main types of life insurance policy: **term life insurance** and **whole of life insurance.** In both cases, the cost of the monthly premium will depend on age, health, including any pre-existing medical conditions, and the sum insured. Term policies only have value during the term of the policy, so if you had a 20-year term and claimed during this, then you get a pay-out. If something happens after the term has ended, then there is no pay-out and no accrued benefit. These are the cheapest policies to buy and are to be taken out to cover you for the period in which you experience the most risk. A good example is while you have a mortgage, if the term of the debt is 25 years then your insurance should match this term. Or, if you have a new baby, they should be financially independent by 21 so this is the term when there is most risk and the policy term should match this.

While most **term life insurance** policies have **fixed premiums for the duration** of the policy, others are **reviewable** policies, where the cost of the premiums can change over time. Every five years, insurance companies examine reviewable policies and may increase the premiums. At this point, if they have increased then many people have to decide between their lifestyle and insurance, and sometimes cancel their policies. To keep the policy in force and ensure there is still some cover, which is better than none, premiums can be fixed or reduced by decreasing the amount insured or the term of the policy to retain the same amount of cover.

A **joint life** policy that covers a couple is usually less expensive than two **single life** policies as it only insures one event for one amount. However, remember that when the first claim is made, the policy ends, so the remaining person will need to seek life insurance separately, if still required.

An interesting benefit of modern insurance is the variety of extra **value-added benefits** which are often offered with life insurance policies at no additional cost. They can include health and wellbeing services such as access to a **virtual doctor** 24/7 without having to wait for an appointment. A virtual GP can be very useful when you are travelling overseas because you can get an instant opinion as to what may be wrong with you if you fall ill. The GP won't be able to prescribe any medication, but they can give a provisional diagnosis as to what you are likely to be suffering from, recommend what to ask for at a local pharmacist and suggest you take urgent action if they are concerned. Policies may also offer a **second medical opinion** from the best doctors in the world for the policyholder, their partner and any children. Some offer access to the best treatments in the world including, for example, global access to cancer care or organ matching in the case of an essential organ transplant. There can also be support for mental health and free annual health check-ups. Some insurance companies offer a range of rewards to encourage people to improve their health and to maintain their fitness levels, such as discounts on gym membership and fitness trackers. I sometimes find that people who are uncertain about taking out life insurance see lots of value when they hear about these added benefits! Do the sums on the benefits as I've had clients who were paying for actual benefits such as a virtual private GP but they switched to insurance to provide this and the plan became a value added benefit that ensures a generous tax free legacy payment for their children.

Level, increasing and decreasing cover

A term life insurance policy pays out a lump sum if a person dies within the term of the policy. If they are still alive at the end of the term, the policy ends and has no cash value. This is why it is cheaper than whole of life insurance and can be a more affordable option for many people as you only cover the need for a specific period while it exists.

Term life insurance policies can last between five and 50 years, depending on your age when you take out the policy. It is up to you to decide the length of the term. Your decision may come down to the cost of premiums. The longer the term, the higher the premiums, because the company is insuring the policyholder for a longer period and people are more likely to die for every year they are alive.

With a **level term** policy, the level of cover and the premiums remain the same throughout the term. This does not take inflation into account so as time passes, the sum insured will have less value in terms of its purchasing power. This should be borne in mind when deciding on the level of cover.

Under an **increasing term** policy, the level of cover increases over the term of the insurance to ensure it keeps up with inflation. The monthly premiums will rise to take this into account. Hopefully your wages will keep pace with this, but the higher payments may become unaffordable for some people. If the premiums are not kept up, the policy will lapse and there will no longer be cover in place. Please note, you can stop the increase on the anniversary of any policy should you want to, or if the increases become unaffordable.

By contrast, the level of cover in a **decreasing term** policy reduces over time but the premiums stay the same. This type of policy is often used to cover a mortgage or other loan where the amount of money owed decreases as the debt is paid off. The policy is no longer needed once a mortgage is paid off, unless a new mortgage is taken out or perhaps you insure a gift for inheritance planning and cover it for the 7-year term for which it remains in the estate. This is technically called a **gift inter vivos** policy, but in effect, it's just another term policy protecting a specific need for a specific term.

A **family income benefit** policy is effectively a combination of level term and decreasing term. It's designed to mimic the need for income. If the policyholder dies while the policy is in force, their family will receive monthly or annual payments until the end of the term instead of a lump sum. For example, if you took out a 20-year policy paying £20,000 a year to your dependants and died 10 years into the policy, your dependants would receive £20,000 for the remaining 10 years of the policy. For every year that you survive, the total payout to dependants will be less, so from the insurers' point of view this is a form of decreasing term policy. It's worth remembering that if the death of the policyholder occurs towards the end of the term, the family will not receive many payments. However, the term of the policy can reflect the period during which the family would most have need of the income. A family income benefit policy is one of the most affordable forms of life insurance and it can be incredibly useful for families or individuals who are on a budget.

A **whole of life** insurance policy does exactly what it says on the tin. It lasts for a person's whole life as long as the premiums are kept up, and it is guaranteed to pay out when they die, so it is more expensive than level term cover. Over a lifetime, personal circumstances and requirements are bound to change, so it is wise to keep an eye on a whole of life insurance policy to make sure it still offers the required level of cover. In most cases, the premiums will need to increase over time so that the sum insured keeps up with inflation, but this isn't a prerequisite.

A whole of life insurance policy is often set up to provide a legacy for children but is often used to cover an expected IHT bill. With increasing property prices, more and more families are finding the value of their estates will be above the nil rate band, and a life insurance plan can be used to cover the amount of IHT payable in part or in full. This often leads to a lower price paid to cover the tax as the premiums are typically lower over the term than the eventual tax and also allow further planning later in life to then provide a legacy lump sum to dependants. For example, if you can afford the premiums and effectively reduce your effective rate of IHT from 40% down to 20% without having to gift anything away or change your lifestyle, then why wouldn't you do this? Inheritance planning is a specialist area, so it is well worth taking advice from an expert.

Critical illness cover

Insurance for **critical illness** has evolved over recent decades in response to advances in medical science. It is designed to provide a lump sum if someone develops a serious illness. However, it is important to check the small print because this type of policy will only cover a specified list of conditions, and the list varies from insurer to insurer.

The top three serious health conditions that critical illness cover pays out for are heart attacks, strokes and cancer. Other serious illnesses covered typically include multiple sclerosis, Parkinson's, MS and ME, plus loss of sight, loss of limbs, deafness and many more.

> **Consider:** *What would you do if you or your partner suffered a critical illness? Would you need to dip into savings earmarked for other things, stop saving, struggle to pay your mortgage or have to retire later?*

If the condition someone has is not on the list, the policy will not pay out. A good example is cancer: only certain types of cancer are included on most insurers' lists of critical illnesses. Skin cancer, for example, is a serious condition, but it is highly treatable in the early stages, so it is unlikely to be covered at the early stage as it may not be critical. When a condition is included, the severity level built into the policy might mean there will be a smaller payout for a less severe form of the illness; this is becoming a more common benefit associated with these plans. In these instances, the policy will often allow multiple claims for that condition until the full amount of the sum insured has been paid out if conditions reoccur.

When an illness is deemed to be critical, cover will normally pay out once for the full amount, and the policy **will end after a successful claim**. If you were to claim for a serious heart attack, for example, the policy would come to an end and you would then need to take out a new policy. The same rule applies to joint policies if either of the insured makes a successful claim. However, there is an exception for claims on behalf of children. Many critical illness policies offer **free cover for children** aged between 1 month and 18 years (21 years if they are still in full-time education) of up to £25,000 per child. This can be a huge benefit for families, and because the policy will usually continue if a claim has to be made for a child, the parents can still make a claim for themselves in the future. This gives parents the option to take time off work to go to medical appointments, pay for specialists or buy specialist equipment to help recovery.

You can usually choose between level cover, decreasing cover or increasing cover for a critical illness policy to meet your exact requirements. This cover can often be seen as expensive, but that is because you are three times more likely to get a critical illness during the term of a plan than you are to die. If you have a limited budget it is wise to insure for an amount that will cover at least two years of your normal outgoings. Many people now survive a critical illness, but during that time their family may want to take a break from work or support them with certain new facilities at home to aid recovery. This amount then ensures that when the worst happens, money isn't a problem in the medium term and all effort can be spent on beating the illness. There are various things that people might choose to do with a payout in practice in addition to covering lost income and paying the mortgage and regular bills. They might want to cover a partner's lost income if they have taken time off work to care for them, pay for a luxury holiday for all the family to recuperate or pay for specialist treatment for their illness (see below for information about specific private medical insurance).

It can be cheaper to **add life insurance to a critical illness policy** but, again, the cover **will only pay out once in either**

event. After a successful claim for critical illness **the policy will end, including the life insurance.** If life insurance is still needed, a separate policy will be required. For some people, a stand-alone critical illness policy is better suited to their needs.

For a critical illness policy to pay out, the policyholder needs to survive for a specified period after the diagnosis, typically 14 days. When a claim is made, a note from a GP or consultant will be needed and medical records will be shared with the insurer, which is why it is important to always tell the truth about your health on insurance application forms. In cases where it is proved that someone has misled the insurance company, the policy is deemed invalid and there will be no payout. A great deal is covered in modern policies as insurers have become more experienced and the industry has matured. **Always disclose information at the underwriting stage so that you know the policy will pay out when you need it to.**

Private medical insurance

Many people choose to take out private medical insurance. Policies are available for individuals and also for families, including parents and their children. For medical emergencies, the NHS is always the first port of call because it is well known for great critical care. But if there's a long waiting list to see a specialist, you can be seen more quickly by 'going private' and claiming back the cost via a private medical insurance policy. This offers more choice and puts you in control of your own health. For example, painful muscular issues can be treated effectively with physiotherapy which can be readily accessed through private medical insurance. The main benefits associated with this insurance are choice, speed of treatment and accountability of the provider.

Income protection

An **income protection** policy can provide peace of mind for people who know they and their family would struggle financially if they were off sick and unable to work for up to 12 months or even longer. Income protection provides cover for people when they cannot work because of illness or injury; this includes both the employed and self-employed. These policies pay out if you can't do your current occupation and will pay until you either go back to work or until the end of the policy, which is typically your retirement date when pensions can be accessed.

Anyone who does not have financial independence – having sufficient money to be able to stop working – should really consider taking out income protection. Those who can't work are not earning, which means they also can't save and put money away for when they actually want to stop working.

Income protection allows them to maintain their lifestyle, pay the mortgage, any school fees etc. and continue saving. Most importantly, it allows them to take stock and recover properly from an illness and return to work only when they feel better. The plans will also typically pay out if you suffer a critical illness that prevents you from working, the definition needed for the payout is simply that you can't continue working in your occupation, which is often the case with critical illness, even in the early stages.

Income protection is a form of sick pay and it provides a supplementary income of between 60% and 70% of a person's gross income for a set period of time. The reason for the limit is because this is the typical level of take-home pay after tax. The idea is that you shouldn't be better off on an insurance payout than when you are when working!

Many employers offer a company sick pay scheme that includes a set number of weeks' full pay, followed by a period of half-pay before your sick leave finally becomes unpaid. If there is no company sick pay scheme, most employees are entitled to statutory sick pay (SSP) for a maximum of 28 weeks. However, the rate is only £109.40 a week (as of April 2023), certainly not enough to live on. Anyone who is still off sick after 28 weeks would have to apply for Employment and Support Allowance instead.

Many people simply would not have sufficient savings to cover the difference between their standard weekly pay and statutory sick pay, especially if they are unwell for any length of time. Income protection helps to plug this gap and means you won't have to use all your hard-earned savings while you're off sick.

> **Consider:** *most people have an emergency fund of 3-6 months' worth of their monthly spending. What would you do if this ran out and you still couldn't work due to illness or injury?*

I like to ask people a simple question: "If you had a machine that pumped out £50 notes in your house, would you insure it?" The answer is typically a resounding yes. The reality is that we are like the money-printing machine, because we work and earn income. If we can't work, then the income stops. Why wouldn't you insure this? You are five times more likely to be off sick than to get a critical illness so, out of all forms of insurance, this is the one that is most likely to pay out – and also will pay if you have a critical illness.

A feature of income protection is the **deferred period** (between 4 weeks and 104 weeks) during which no benefits are paid from the policy. This is designed to take into account any company sick pay scheme you may be entitled to, so you can choose to wait until a specific date for benefits to kick in. The longer the deferred period, the cheaper the premiums. So if you are entitled to three months sick pay from your employer, then you have a three month deferred period before the policy kicks in to take over.

For self-employed people without access to a company sick pay scheme, it is advisable to have a three-month emergency cash fund (as discussed in the chapter on Savings). They can then opt for a deferred period of 12 weeks, which will be far less expensive than needing payments from day one.

Unlike critical illness cover, income protection pays out if someone cannot work because of **almost any illness**, including mental health conditions. Maybe they have had a car accident and the recovery period is long. Or they have developed a long-term health condition that affects their work. Perhaps a family member is going through a serious illness and this could adversely affect the policyholder's own mental health. Dealing with that level of stress at the same time as working is extremely difficult. In modern life, we are constantly putting ourselves under strain and pressure, and eventually we will break. In all these cases, income protection will pay out. Mental strain such as stress is the top illness to pay out, followed by a bad back.

There are **short-term** income protection policies, which typically pay out **between 12 and 18 months**, or **long-term** policies that last **until retirement.** Most people go back to work within 18 months, though they might relapse later. The beauty of income protection policies is that **multiple claims can be made during the term** – as many as are needed.

Calculating the amount of income protection cover to take out is relatively easy. If someone earns £2,000 a month net of tax, they should cover themselves for that amount. Ideally, they should add in inflation-proofing so that premiums and the payout go up in line with inflation every year. The claim can be in force for up to two years at a time. People don't have to cover their full income – they can opt for a lower amount if you want, or they can have a level of cover that will pay out until they retire. But the term of the cover always dictates the premium.

It is worth considering adding a **waiver of premium** benefit to any protection policy. Under this benefit, the insurer pays the monthly premiums when you cannot work after 26 weeks due to illness, and the cover is maintained.

As with critical illness cover, when a claim is made, a note from your GP is required and they will share your medical records with the insurer. Around 70% of all claims for income protection are accepted.

As part of the policy, there is a lot of useful support to get people back to work. If a person can no longer carry out the occupation they followed when they took out income protection, they might be able to go back to work in a different role or a new occupation. Someone on £50,000 a year who has been suffering with stress might choose to work part-time, or take a job paying a lower salary but with fewer responsibilities. The policy is designed to encourage people to try and get back to work because it gives them a purpose in life. If the new job pays less, the income protection benefit (known as **proportionate benefit**) will pay the difference. A proportionate benefit is also paid to top up someone's salary with a proportion of the monthly benefit if they return to work at a reduced capacity. There is also usually rehabilitation support to help people return to their job more quickly, for example, physio sessions for physical injuries, or therapy for mental illness.

Over-50s insurance

Over-50s insurance is a specific type of insurance that does not require a medical. People with these policies pay set monthly premiums and are guaranteed a lump sum payout when they die. These plans are typically sold as a way of paying for funeral costs so that loved ones do not have to worry about covering that expense, and they typically provide cover for a maximum of £10,000.

It's important to note that premiums do not keep up with inflation so they may not provide sufficient money to pay the whole cost of a funeral. The other main issue is that policyholders could get back far less than they paid in, depending on their age when the policy was started. Over-50s insurance plans are not usually the best value, so it's worth checking with a financial adviser first.

Long-term care insurance

Older people who can no longer perform the activities of daily living (ADL) independently may need long-term help from carers, either in their own homes or in a care home. This care comes at a significant cost, but there is currently no specific insurance policy that people can take out to cover their future long-term care.

Instead, some insurance companies offer **immediate needs annuities**, also known as immediate care plans, that can be bought with a lump sum. As the monthly payments from the annuity **go directly to the care provider**, they are not classed as income, so they are **not taxable**. This means more of the money goes towards the cost of care. One issue with this type of insurance is that for some plans, if a person dies not long after purchasing the annuity, they won't get any money back. However, guarantees can be added to these plans at an additional cost if required. Another thing to be aware of is the danger of rapid increases in the cost of care and potential longevity in care, which means that an annuity may not be able to meet these fully over time.

This is a very specialist area, so it is wise to take professional advice. Payments from long-term care insurance may affect some means-tested benefits. A financial advisor can explain the pros and cons and the best options for individual circumstances.

Business protection

There are a couple of main policies to consider for business owners which are often set up as term policies and paid for by the company. They can usually cover life or critical illness but there are also corporate income protection policies available. **Key person** cover is designed to pay the company in the event of the death or critical illness of a key employee. The company can then use the proceeds to cover the cost of hiring someone to replace the Key person or cover any loss of profits they would typically produce. **Shareholder and Partnership** protection simply pays the company a lump sum equal to the value of the deceased shareholder's or partner's shares in the company. They use this money to acquire the shares of the deceased person and provide the financial proceeds to the deceased's estate. The family typically don't want to be involved in the business but need the financial value and the company simply want to continue to work as they have before.

Shortcuts

Life insurance

- The **younger & typically healthier** you are when you take out a policy, the **cheaper** the premiums.

- It's often cheaper to **amend or extend an existing policy** rather than taking out a new one, so taking out a life policy when you are younger is always a good idea.

- Always check your **employment benefits** for **death in service**, sickness and critical illness before taking out other insurance, as these are 'free' and tax efficient. Remember they are not transferable if you change companies at a later date.

- **Term life insurance** covers you for a fixed period and expires at the end of the term; premiums may be **reviewable** at fixed intervals and are likely to increase, at which point it is possible to fix or reduce premiums by reducing levels of cover or the policy term. Take out policies with **guaranteed premiums** at the start to avoid any future increases.

- **Value added benefits** to life insurance policies, such as virtual GPs and 'best doctor' second medical opinions, can be very valuable.

- **Whole life insurance** is guaranteed to pay out on death, so is more expensive than a simple term plan.

- Life insurance can be **level, increasing** or **decreasing** term. Match this to your specific need to keep ensure your policy pays out what you need in the future if you need to make a claim. Indexing your policy ensures it **keeps pace with**

inflation, premiums will increase with inflation but typically your income will increase above this.

Critical illness cover

- Critical illness policies will cover a **range of specified conditions;** if a condition is on the list you get paid out, if not on the list, you will not be covered. These policies will all cover the most common illnesses and are designed to pay out, typically 90% of all claims are for cancer, heart attacks and strokes.

- Different **levels of severity** of illness can receive different levels of pay-out.

- Policies **end after a successful claim** and you will need to start a new policy.

- Most policies provide free critical illness in **children between one month and 18 years** (21 years if still in full-time education); a claim for a child's illness **does not affect any future claims on behalf of the parents** themselves.

- **Private medical insurance** covers individuals or families for the use of private medical care. It provides the benefits of choice and speed of treatment more than anything else.

Income protection insurance

- The longer the **deferred period** before income protection payments are made, the **cheaper** the premiums are.

Match this to your sick pay levels and emergency fund (3-6 months) to keep premiums down.

- Always check with your **employer** to see what **existing cover** may be in place.

- Income protection covers **almost any illness, including mental health** if you are unable to work.

- Cover can be **short term,** typically up to **12 or 18 months,** or **long term,** covering the insured until **retirement** age. The average period for any claim is under 2 years before people go back to work.

- **Multiple claims** can be made during the term of the policy and this doesn't change or affect the policy or premiums.

- Always add additional waiver of premiums benefit, so cover is maintained if you can't afford premiums during an illness.

- **Proportionate benefits** may be payable if you return to work on a lower salary or do a different job as you are unable to do your previous occupation due to illness or injury.

- Buy one less coffee each day and use this saving to insure yourself and your family properly.

Chapter 8: Investment

Most of us at some point will want to save for something bigger and better and to grow our wealth. To do that, we will need to invest. Cash is not risk free as it needs to keep pace with inflation and Investing is inherently risky; the value of investments are based upon the subjective value we place on them, so some people shy away from it. But risk is not necessarily a bad thing. Life itself is risky, but that doesn't stop us living it! In order to have a better chance of higher, longer-term returns, investors need to accept a level of risk. There is a delicate balance between risk and reward, but if that balance is achieved, the potential returns can be lucrative.

Before starting to invest, it is essential to have sufficient **cash reserves** in the form of savings available to meet short-term needs, including any emergencies. This is fundamental to provide a solid foundation before we think about taking on risk. Without that foundation, it is easy to be too demanding of our investments, looking to make quick returns – taking on too much risk and making more emotionally-laden decisions. Cash is one option for trying to grow wealth, but it is not risk free as it needs to keep pace with inflation in order to grow in value. Typically it will do this, but only by a small margin. It tends to keep pace with inflation more than grow beyond it and so this won't produce the best returns over the long term.

If we plan to spend money on something we want in the next few years, that money should come from our savings (cash). The main return here is access to capital and security because the money is already earmarked for spending and so you don't want to speculate with this saved money. But if someone has a financial goal that is **more than five years away,** they should be investing rather than saving more cash. This means they can afford to go through periods where the economic cycle might be down, because they are looking at the picture over the longer term. Economic cycles tend to follow a five- to seven-year cycle and the value of most investments follow suit.

One of the key points to remember is that the longer you tie up your money for, the better the return. Typically, you sacrifice access for better returns. You will have more capacity to take risk and weather temporary losses but, obviously, you will also have less access to ready cash. This is why the **timeframe** for investments is so important and needs to be tailor-made to suit investors' individual requirements. You don't want to be in the position where you are forced to cash in investments at the bottom of an economic cycle.

The good news, as I say, is that investments have always delivered good results in the long term. Investments in equities, for example, have a **75% chance of outperforming cash** over 5 years, a **95% chance** over **10** years and a **99% chance** over **15** years. This is why they are the default choice for pension funds.

If someone had invested **£100,000** back in **1987**, they would need to have approximately **£300,000** today to match the value of the original £100,000 after **inflation**. If they had put all their money in **cash**, they would have about **£450,000 today**. If they had invested in **bonds**, they would have about **£1 million**. If they had put the money into property or the stock market, they would have about **£1.8 million**. We will talk about the key aspects of these different types of investment, such as bonds, equities and property in a moment. With hindsight, putting every single penny in stocks and property back in 1987 would have been the best decision, but investors don't have the benefit of hindsight. Making investment choices is never easy, and it would have been a rollercoaster ride along the way, even with those wonderful final returns. I'll discuss the psychology of money in a later chapter and look at the skills and considerations needed to remain invested and manage behaviour to remain invested. **Time in the market delivers over the long term.** (See chart at end of chapter.)

The risk spectrum

One of the main risks of investing is that your investments could **fall in value**. In fact, this is a certainty during some periods. But over time they will go up more often than they will go down, depending on the type of investment. Investors need to be comfortable enough to withstand some losses for a period. They need to consider their capacity for loss and how much they are willing to lose. If someone has invested everything they have and if they absolutely need those investments to go up in value in order to achieve a future goal, that means they have invested too much. In an ideal world, you should only invest only money that you can theoretically afford to lose.

I'm not suggesting that you are going to lose all your investments, but there will be times when the value of those investments is less than you hoped – or possibly less than you initially invested. It helps greatly if you are able to invest in a state of mind that accepts that if you lost all of your investment in the worst possible scenario, you would still be able to maintain your current lifestyle. In practice, of course, it is virtually impossible to lose all of your investments, unless you put all of your money into one vehicle: shares in just one company, for example, and that company then goes bust. We will talk about the diversification of investments in a moment. But literally any kind of investment carries a degree of risk.

Wherever investors are on the risk spectrum determines the **level of risk** they are willing to take which essentially means the level of volatility, how much the value of their investment can move up and down. In terms of rising potential returns in exchange for rising levels of risk, their investments will typically rise in volatility starting with in **cash**, then **bonds**, then **property** and then **shares**. Higher-risk investments might include more exposure to overseas elements, speculating on currency fluctuations, or concentrating risks into a single category, share, property or geographic region.

The irony is that the more money someone has, the less risk they need to take. After a certain point, increasing their wealth makes no real difference because it doesn't physically impact their current lifestyle, or even their future lifestyle. Those with far less money often try taking more risks to achieve big goals, which can lead to problems if they overstretch themselves. Everyone else (most of us!) lies somewhere between these two extremes.

It is possible to **reduce risk** in a number of ways, but the simplest is through **diversification**: investing across a range of different **asset classes** and not putting all available eggs in one basket, and also using investment managers who are skilled at choosing investments, rather than investing on a do-it-yourself basis.

The more diversification there is in an investment portfolio, the lower the risk, the lower the volatility and the smoother the returns. Riskier investments can deliver better returns in the long-term but, obviously, some of those riskier investments will also underperform or even fail, and cost money in the short term. It's important also to not over diversify. If you buy too much of everything then you take out all the risk, and can forgo potentially much higher returns over the long term.

The further away people are in time from their financial goals, the more risk they can afford to take. The closer they are to retirement age, the more cautious they might choose to be with their investments because they physically have less working years remaining and therefore less time to catch up if things go down, so they want less volatility and risk at that point.

Types of investment

As we have discussed, it is difficult to make spectacular returns on cash savings, even during periods of increasing interest rates. We talked in the chapter on Savings about the effect of inflation, and how it is essential that our savings and investments outperform inflation. Cash savings, in general, may keep pace with inflation but are unlikely to outperform it significantly. Investments offer the opportunity of allowing our money to deliver real, inflation-busting growth.

There are three major asset classes that people can invest in: bonds, shares ('equities') and property.

Bonds are a form of investment in which people lend money to a government or company in return for a fixed rate of interest during the term of the bond, getting their capital back at the end of the term. The loan is typically secured to the value of assets and so you effectively become a form of interest-only mortgage lender.

There are two typical types of bonds: **government bonds** and **corporate bonds.**

Government bonds are less risky because governments generate money through taxes and will normally survive, no matter what. What matters most is a country's reputation for repaying its debts. A few years ago, for example, there was a major debt crisis in Greece. Because of this, Greek government bonds were available at about 9% interest and anyone who invested in these bonds got a good return; this is called the risk premium, where there is a higher rate of return from riskier investments. At the same time, the return for investing in UK government bonds was typically 2%. The reason for that is the UK government has never failed to pay back its debts, whereas Greece was in danger of going bankrupt.

Corporate bonds are a way for companies to raise money; if you buy a corporate bond, you are effectively lending that company money in return for the payment of interest. The bond has a term, and when the bond 'matures' the company will pay you back the face value of the bond in addition to the interest you have received. The more established the company issuing the bond, of course, the more certain it is that your loan will be repaid. A bond in a major corporation, such as Ford Motor Company or Apple Inc would be seen, quite rightly, as a safe bet. A bond issued by a startup with no track record would be far riskier, and the interest rate offered would reflect that.

Most companies secure bonds issued against assets that they own (**secured bonds**). Bonds have a defined letter-based **rating** relative to their quality and stability. They start off at AAA, AA, A, BBB, BB, B and so on, through to D (**junk bonds**, classed as non-investment grade). These lower-rated bonds have a higher level of risk, which is why investors are compensated with a higher premium/interest rate. So-called junk bonds can offer excellent returns – but they are also very risky.

Bonds usually pay a **fixed interest payment** (sometimes called a **fixed coupon**) and, like anything of value, bonds can be **traded**. When interest rates are low, bonds become more attractive to investors because they offer a guaranteed return. If I hold a bond offering a competitive return with several years of its term remaining at a time when interest rates in general are low, someone may offer to buy that bond off me for more than I paid for it. In these circumstances, the price of bonds in general goes up. But if I hold a bond paying a low rate of interest at a time when interest rates are rising, I might be keen to sell it, because new bonds are being issued at higher rates of interest as the issuers try to stay competitive. In these circumstances, the price of bonds in general goes down. But as the value of a bond falls, so the **yield** (interest) it pays becomes a higher percentage of the bond's value. If interest rates begin to fall, that lower-priced bond with its relatively high yield begins to look more attractive, and so demand increases and values rise. This simple logic drives the **bond market.** Bond markets can be a little tricky to understand because they tend to have an inverse relationship to interest rates: as interest rates rise, so bond markets tend to fall.

Some experienced investors choose to buy and sell bonds which have different maturities. This allows them to utilise the yield curve, a line on a graph that plots the interest rates of bonds with different maturity dates but equal credit quality. A bond's **duration** is a measure of its sensitivity to interest rates. The closer it is to the end of the term, the less sensitive the bond is to interest rates. This is because you get all your capital back, so even if rates go up or down, so long as you hold the bond then you get all your money back so the risk is much lower.

Bonds should typically outperform cash in terms of inflation, but the volatility range is a lot lower then equities or property. Investors can typically expect to outperform cash savings by around 1.5%, and realise around a 4% p.a. return on bonds in the longer term.

Equities are **shares** in a company that are traded on **stock markets** across the world. The biggest stock market is the US, which typically holds about 50% of all stocks. The UK equates to only about 4% of the global market, but the London Stock Exchange is one of the oldest exchanges and is still a leading player. If you are based in the UK, there are advantages in buying equities in the UK to avoid the complications of currency fluctuations.

Before investing, I always ask people if they believe in evolution. Why? Because if you do then you understand the idea of the survival of the fittest and that this provides stronger and better versions of everything. The cream always rises to the top. In markets this is an incredibly efficient process as there is no emotion involved in it. Whatever we do as people in the world requires companies to facilitate it. We buy goods or services in energy, technology, industry, commodities, food, housing, health and recreation pretty much every day of our lives, as these are all things we need and each industry just gets better over time as they compete for our business. Companies innovate, and we use our collective purchasing power to buy the goods and services of the best ones. This competition encourages progress and innovation and so over time the best companies in the world at any time provide the goods or services which we all love the most. Consider today's top companies, Apple, Tesla and Zoom. These weren't even companies a few decades ago when the world was dominated by tobacco and oil companies. We change, and so do the places we spend our money. We evolve and if you continue to invest in the world's best businesses then they will continue to evolve too.

As a useful rule of thumb, the long-term average rate of return from investments in equities is 5.5% p.a. In good years, investors might get 20% or 30% returns on stock markets. In bad years, of course, there can be losses of the same magnitude. Stocks can be traded almost instantly, which makes them very volatile. Stock markets are notoriously prone to 'panics' that are often quickly over, but there are also genuine 'crashes', typically after periods of dramatic but ultimately unjustifiable growth, normally described as 'bubbles'.

Nevertheless, the striking thing about stock markets in the long term is that there are a lot more positive years than negative ones. Over the past 100 years, the US stock market has only delivered a negative return for one year in every four and the overall trend in stock market value has been a steady and significant upwards climb. Global markets typically go up 75% of the time and down 25% of the time. Over the longer term things go up more than they go down and so over time you just get more good years than bad years.

Most people buy stocks in companies that are listed on the open market as **public limited companies (PLCs)**. Anyone in the world can buy these stocks. The level of available data about these businesses is extremely detailed. The skill lies in digesting and deciphering the data to fully understand what a company's stock is worth. There are various tools for estimating this, the most common of which is the **price to earnings ratio (P/E)** – the relationship between a company's earnings per share in the form of profits and the current value of its stock. If a company has a share value of $100 per share and its earnings per share are $10, for example, it has a P/E ratio of 10. This can be a useful guide – companies with a surprisingly high P/E ratio might well be undervalued, in which case their share price could be expected to rise over time. However, some exciting new companies (especially in the technology sector, for example) may not have any earnings at all in their early years. Other companies may be investing heavily, keeping current earnings (profits) low, even though they may perform very well in the future as a result. The P/E ratio is useful but, of course, if it was an infallible guide, we would all be rich! The fact that a stock seems 'cheap', doesn't guarantee that it will go up in price. The fact that something seems 'over-priced', by the same token, doesn't guarantee it will go down in price. Stock selection is a highly complex area, which is why people prefer to let expert fund managers or fund houses do this for them.

It is possible to invest in '**unlisted**' businesses: companies that are not listed on any stock market and which are owned outright by people running their own companies. These companies can be incredibly successful, but they don't have to publish their data and they can sell shares privately. It is very risky to invest in unlisted businesses because it is difficult for most people to value them accurately. Most investments of this kind occur when there is a personal connection: the company is owned by a family member, a close acquaintance, or there is another company in the same trade looking to grow and the investor or company decides to take a chance on its potential by buying shares. One key issue is that, because there is no stock market valuation of the company, its shares are worth only what someone else will pay for them. If you want to sell them, you will have to find a willing buyer and hope that they will pay a premium on your original price. The ideal scenario would be if the company you now own shares in were to 'go public', listing its shares on the stock market, in which case your shares could become very valuable indeed.

With equities, investors benefit from returns in two ways:

through **capital appreciation**, where the stock price increases in value, and through **dividends**, where companies choose to pay a proportion of its overall profits to their shareholders. Companies are not obliged to pay dividends, and the amount paid is also entirely discretionary. UK equities tend to pay dividends more than, for example, US and China equities. Some European stocks also pay good dividends, depending on the industry sector. Some investors choose equities more as a source of regular dividend income than for any major capital appreciation. As the value of the company increases over time then the dividends will also increase as they are paid as a percentage of share value. This can be a good option for those seeking long term income to keep pace with inflation.

The concept of 'survival of the fittest' is fully reflected in equities. Companies that evolve in the ever-changing marketplace thrive and flourish. Companies that fail to adapt to shifting consumer demands quicky go under. There will always be reliable consumer staples such as energy companies and makers of toilet paper and toothpaste. Such companies tend to be very well-managed, and they can be relied on to deliver steady, if not dramatic, growth. But other new businesses start up every day that might become the next top-performing company of tomorrow. It is a fast-moving, unflinching marketplace.

Because markets are driven by real human beings, they are also influenced by fads and trends. The last decade was all about technology businesses; before that the market was focussed on energy stocks. There was a phase when Japanese companies were experiencing phenomenal growth and were all the rage. And they may well be again; everything has its time in the sun. These trends are most significant when they are driven by real consumer demand. There are other times when markets get over-excited about a new development that seems to be 'the next big thing', and share prices get inflated beyond any sensible reckoning of their genuine value, leading to bubbles. The dot.com bubble at the turn of the millennium is a classic example, when understandable excitement about the potential of the internet led to many early internet companies being given totally unrealistic valuations. In the end this played out correctly as the tech boom arrived and the businesses that were delivering the most useful services proved their worth.

Property is a very interesting asset and one that most people understand. Most investments are in residential property, but commercial property can also offer an interesting investment opportunity

In the **residential property** market, the main driver of prices is the ability to obtain credit. Very few people can buy a property outright so lower interest rates mean they can borrow more on a mortgage. The cheaper the cost of the debt, the less it costs to borrow money, so the more people will borrow. Another driver is the availability of property. As the population increases, there is more demand for accommodation which increases property prices, especially on a crowded island like the UK.

One way of investing in residential properties is to 'flip' them by selling them on, especially after adding value to them. That can be quite costly because of the taxes involved in buying property ('stamp duty'), and it can take several months to sell a property. Within that time, these investors can experience both buyers' and sellers' remorse, which can affect the way they handle their investment.

Investing in a buy-to-let is a bit of a postcode lottery. Some areas do really well because they are in demand. Others have quite weak rental markets. For property, the average long-term growth is 4% or 5% a year. With a buy-to-let, there will be income in the form of rent, as well as capital growth. Higher taxation over the last decade has been a headwind to some investors' returns but this still remains a solid wealth builder and diversifier.

Buy-to-lets can be time-consuming for the investor because there is an ongoing process of setting rents, renewing leases and/or finding new tenants and keeping the property well-maintained. As mentioned, property is one of the most illiquid assets because it can take months to buy and sell, so it is very difficult if access to ready cash is needed. But some of the benefits of the smooth returns on property arise precisely because of this **lack of liquidity.**

Commercial property, which includes retail outlets, warehousing and office space, is slightly different. During the pandemic, the office sector suffered, although a lot of them were still occupied, albeit less busy than before. There are also retail units on high streets, warehouses and light industrial properties. Commercial properties have longer leases than residential properties, meaning they deliver a reliable return for a longer period. Commercial property has traditionally been seen as a low-risk investment, though recent changes to the way we shop – especially the rise of online shopping – have raised doubts about the future of the traditional high street. But businesses will always need premises, and these will always centre around where people live, and the sector will also always evolve around our needs. One major stumbling block in this sector is the high level of acquisition costs and borrowing. Many investors decide to invest in a fund instead of directly owning commercial property in order to access this asset class without over-concentrating their investments.

Alternative investments

There are several other more 'niche' investment opportunities, for all of which professional advice is recommended. **Absolute return funds** aim to deliver a return to investors regardless of the current performance of the market. Investors can also include **commodities** in their portfolios, which are most commonly bought into as managed funds. Commodities are raw materials such as oil, gas, wood, gold and silver, and primary agricultural products such as coffee, beans and wheat. There are also **exchange traded funds (ETFs)**, which track the performance of a commodity or an industry sector. More complex investment strategies include hedging currencies and the use of derivatives, all of which are the province of specialist advisors; the average investor will focus on cash, bonds, major equities and property.

The behaviour of markets

A simple way to understand markets is to liken them to sprints and rest periods. If someone sprinted to the end of their road, that would be the equivalent of the daily or weekly spurts of a market trend. By the time they reached the end, they would be out of breath and would need to recover, but not for long. This recovery times is the equivalent of the markets going down for a short period. When they have regained energy, they can sprint again and can keep doing these short sprints for quite a while.

But the longer they do it for, it effectively becomes a marathon. If they ran like this for long periods, they would become exhausted and experience a big drop in energy, and the recovery takes a lot longer. That is the equivalent of the big 'corrections' to markets that happen after long periods of growth. They run out of steam and need to rest. Once exhaustion passes, the market is ready to go again, and is often stronger for it.

When markets start recovering after these downturns, people find it hard to believe that this will be sustainable. But markets are forward-looking, and they tend to reflect what is expected to be the reality six months in the future. Experienced stock pickers and fund managers start to buy stocks that they know are undervalued and represent good value. It's important to remember that companies are run by people and they don't like pain, so when things are not going well, they do something about it: they innovate, create plans, find solutions to problems and then put all their efforts into this. As significant shareholders, fund managers get direct access to the CEOs and top management teams of companies, so they know the strategies and can look in the eyes of the people who will turn things around. As the price starts to rise, people begin to take notice and gain confidence, start to buy, and the price continues to increase. In 9-12 months' time, the markets are often back to where the experts predicted.

There are many amazing businesses to invest in, but people are unsure how to value them. Valuing companies accurately is never straightforward. META, for example, which used to be Facebook, lost 65% of its value in 2022 but it is still a phenomenal business. Many big tech businesses lost 50% or more, and even Amazon and Apple lost 28%. Stock pickers understand the value of companies because they use balance sheets, and they talk to the managers and the people who run the businesses, but even they can be caught out by unexpected moves in the market. The tech market, for example, has been more affected by recent rises in interest rates than had been expected. The total value of stock markets will always be increasing because companies evolve to meet the demand for their goods and services from the growing population, and because inflation increases the price of goods. The value will always go up, but it does not go up evenly and not always at the same rate. There are always winners and losers in every sector.

We talked about market bubbles and sudden enthusiasm for what is seen to be 'the next big thing.' A good recent example of this is **cryptocurrency**. There is definitely a value to cryptocurrency, but no one is quite sure what that value is. It is very similar to the Dutch 'tulip mania' financial crash of the seventeenth century, when tulips were all the rage and the bulbs of especially attractive varieties began to change hands at ridiculous prices. At the height of the bubble, bulbs were being sold for the price of a house. When this kind of buying mania sets in, people lose sight of the genuine value of what they are buying. Prices are going up so quickly that they are afraid of missing out. Everyone begins to believe that prices will continue to go up and that 'you can't lose.' I met a couple once who fell into this exact trap; they had just sold their house during this market surge and the husband had decided to put the money into crypto instead of cash, as he was convinced he would double the money and buy a dream house. It went up for a small period but then lost 70% of the value in the crash and as a result his wife divorced him. Needless to say, a lot of people come into booming markets very late, when everyone is talking about them. They pay at the top end and then the prices become clearly unjustifiable. The scales fall from people's eyes, and they stop buying. Or sometimes there's an economic issue – some kind of tipping point. The prices start to slide, people panic, and everyone starts to sell. Once the belief sets in, the price drops and drops. These fear periods are very powerful, and they have twice the impact of the optimism felt in a good period.

Imagine walking down the street and finding £50. You're elated! But then imagine losing that £50 later the same day. Although you're neither worse or better off, the pain of losing the money is likely to be greater than the elation you felt when you found it. In economics, this is called **loss aversion**. When people see stock prices falling, they think they are going to lose all their money. They capitulate and panic, selling all their stocks without looking at what is still good in their portfolio, including really solid stocks. That means the value of a lot of good stocks is pulled down along with everything else. These days a high proportion of all trading – perhaps 30% – is caused by tracker funds, which are essentially following the market. Most people are not fully aware of what stocks they are invested in via these funds. If they sell, they are selling the good as well as the bad, so they are selling stocks that might actually be going up in price. There are always winners and losers in all scenarios, even in falling markets. But eventually the price will be so low that people will look at it, think it is really cheap, start to buy it, and the cycle begins all over again.

The first thing investors need to accept is that no one can predict the future. The world goes through different phases and economies are always changing. In 2022-23, Europe struggled because of the war in Ukraine, and Brexit has hampered the UK significantly over the last five or six years. The US has had the benefit of the big tech bubble, China had its big growth phase of exports, and India is experiencing similar growth now.

If one market is going up, another goes down. The ideal would be to use diversification to hedge investments and to smooth out returns. Consumer staples such as toothpaste and washing powder are still bought in recessionary periods. Technology booms when interest rates are low and entrepreneurs can raise inexpensive capital for speculative new ventures. A lot of investing involves thinking about the potential future growth of core business sectors. Investors can diversify across sectors like energy, property and healthcare, for example, because we know that each one of those sectors will have some kind of growth.

There are winners and losers in all these different sectors, and it is quite hard to pick winners. But all investors need to do is pick more winners than losers.

Every investor worries about crashes, because they are so memorable. There was Black Monday (1987); the first Gulf War (1990); the European Exchange Rate Mechanism crisis (1992); the Asian currency crisis (1997); the September 11th attacks (2001); the invasion of Iraq (2003); the collapse of Lehman Brothers (2008); China trade war tensions (2018); and, most recently, the effects of the COVID-19 pandemic in 2020.

These regular crises seem very scary. Our loss aversion and our aversion to pain means that the bad events tend to stick in our mind, and we determine that we will make sure we don't get caught out by them in the future. But markets always recover, and the value of long-term investments continues to rise.

The stock market crash of 1973-74, for example, was one of the worst since the Great Depression, affecting stock markets all around the world. The UK market was particularly badly hit, with 40% to 50% negative returns on equities. That was a one-in-100-year event. Interestingly, the following year was one of the best years ever, as markets picked up again, delivering more than 60% return. The sun always comes out after a storm, and negative years will be followed by positive ones.

The famous investor Warren Buffett says investors should be 'fearful when others are greedy, and greedy when others are fearful'. It has certainly worked for him. In his early years of trading with his own firm, Buffet Partnership Ltd, between 1957 and 1969, he achieved an average 30% return year on year.[6]

Investing Tips

I'd like to offer a few tips on investment. They represent a kind of collective wisdom about investing and you will see the same tips, or different variations on the same theme, in many places, typically because they often make logical sense and work in most scenarios.

The main focus of this section is the **stock market** but in many ways the same theories apply to most subjectively priced investments as all asset classes go through peaks and troughs from time to time.

[6] How Warren Buffet Achieved a 30% Annual Return for 10+ Years | DataDrivenInvestor

The stock market is by definition **volatile**, but it offers **better returns** in the long term. The important thing to note about the stock market is that it is **undefeated**: it has continued to grow in value despite every conceivable shock and upset. In the twentieth century, we have seen two World Wars and many serious conflicts; the Spanish Flu pandemic of 1918-19, which caused up to 50 million deaths worldwide; the Great Depression; more than a dozen recessions; the resignation of presidents and the deaths of kings and queens; Despite all of this turmoil, the stock market is consistently setting new all-time highs, as it has been on roughly 5% of all trading days in the last 100 years – the point being that the market can be set back, but it continues on its long-term upwards trajectory.[7]

You may have heard about '**bear markets**' and '**bull markets**'. Market cycles are measured from peak to trough. The stock index officially reaches bear territory when the closing price drops by 20% from its recent high, and a bull market begins when the closing price rises by 20%.

The S&P 500 index, which tracks the stock prices of 500 of the largest companies trading on US stock exchanges, has recorded 27 bear markets and 27 bull markets since 1928. The average length of bear markets has been **292** days, or nearly 10 months. The average length of bull markets has been **992** days, or 2 years and nearly 9 months. We spend a lot more

[7] Investing in Stocks At All-Time Highs - A Wealth of Common Sense

time in 'bull' territory (75%) than we do in 'bear' territory (25%).

When markets are doing badly – when we are in a bear market – it feels very painful. Everyone's stock holdings have lost value and 10 months (or longer) feels like a long time. It then typically takes about another 10 months for the markets to fully recover, but then the sun shines for maybe another 2 years. If you were to start investing at the beginning of a bear market, you would watch your investment go down in value for many months, perhaps even for a year or more. But eventually the market will rally, and over time you will see a good return on your money. Many people see investing in the stock market as 'risky' because of the volatility and see cash savings as being 'safe'. But inflation eats into the value of cash savings and, over the longer term, investment in the stock market has **massively outperformed cash** savings, as we saw earlier.

It is worth pointing out that any longer-term analysis of the market makes it sound relatively 'smooth': the market goes down for maybe 10 months, then it goes up for maybe 33 months. But there are quite dramatic swings within this longer-term movement. About 42% of the S&P 500 index's strongest days in last 20 years occurred during bear markets, and another 34% of the market's best days took place in the first two months of a bull market.

The lesson to draw from this is that it is very hard to 'double guess' the market. Making the right investment based on short-term movements in the market is incredibly difficult. The wise approach is to get into the market and stay there, and weather the various peaks and troughs. There is a wise saying among investors: **"It's about 'time in' the market, not 'timing' the market."** Many people are fearful about investing when the market is going down, and they wait until they feel they can see the signs of an upturn. But some of the best upturns may happen during a bear market - only to be followed by a rapid downturn. Even professional investors find it impossible to spot the bottom or the top of a market. So the wise answer is: invest for the long term and leave your money in place. In the long term, stocks will be rising about 75% of the time.

Another interesting aspect of the stock market is that investment risks are **asymmetric**. If you invest in a stock, the worst that can happen so that it loses 100% of its value. But the potential upside has no limit. Stocks in Amazon, for example, have risen by over 7000% in the last 20 years. If you had invested £1,000 in Amazon 20 years ago, those stocks would be worth around £78,100 today.[8] Unfortunately, very few people are able to spot only those stocks that will perform well, let alone exceptionally well, and hold them the whole time.

Making investment decisions based on the **news** is also a

[8] How Much Would $10,000 Invested in Amazon Stock 20 Years Ago Be Worth Today? | Investing | U.S. News (usnews.com)

bad idea. There is always something bad going on somewhere in the world; wars break out; there are floods and tornados and hurricanes. The stock market is so responsive that any 'news' like this is almost instantaneously '**priced in**' to the market: traders make their judgment about the likely effect of the event and buy and sell within seconds to reflect that. This means that anything you have heard about in the news is already reflected into today's market price. It's the things you haven't heard about yet that you need to worry about – which is another way of saying that you are highly unlikely to be able to beat the market by following the news and you might as well relax. This is not to say that your gut instinct about long-term trends should be ignored. If you have a view on the industries that are likely to prosper over the next decade or so, you might well be right. But think in decades in this case and not days.

Diversifying your investments across a range of different types of investment is highly recommended. At any one time, some of your portfolio will be down and other parts will be up, but the more diversified you are, the more likely you are to benefit from the market's long-term growth. Some investment funds are designed to follow the market as a whole, which is another way of saying that they are broadly diversified. Other funds specialise in certain areas. Some are designed specifically to offer higher returns, which means that they are also riskier and invest in more volatile stocks. Investing in a range of funds diversifies your own portfolio.

When you know that you need to withdraw money from your investments, try to **plan 12 months ahead** and talk to your advisor if you have one. You don't want to take money out of funds that are doing very well and would be better off taking money out of something 'steadier'. It might be wise to transfer money that you know you will need from a more volatile fund to a less volatile one. In general, to grow your wealth, you will need at least some exposure to more volatile and riskier areas. Once you have built wealth - and almost certainly as you get older - it is a good idea to move money into less volatile areas. It is also a typical trait of the wealthiest investors; they diversify more to minimise loss. If you don't need to take the risk to make money you won't spend, then why risk it?

My key investment tips are listed below. As I say, I can't make any claim for originality, but I can say that I have seen these tips proven to be good advice over the years and when ignored the costs can be high.

1. **Make sure you have an 'emergency fund'** of savings other than your investments. Timing is everything, and you don't want to have to cash in investments at the worst possible moment just because you need money to deal with some unexpected event.

2. **Don't take a short-term view.** It's easy to panic when things are going badly; history tells us that the market will recover, no matter how bad the shock.

3. **Diversify.** Some sectors underperform, some do unexpectedly well; the more diversified your portfolio is, the more you are spreading the risk and smoothing returns.

4. **Accept some losses.** Selling in a panic crystallizes losses in stocks that might well recover in time, but some stocks simply fail to perform over time. Sell up, accept your losses and move on. Ask yourself the question, if I didn't own this today, would I buy it now? Your answer should clarify your next move.

5. **Learn from your mistakes.** History doesn't always repeat itself, but it certainly does rhyme; if you get burned by one scenario, it's best to avoid similar scenarios in future unless you've learnt from it. Look to why things went wrong and if there were any obvious signs in hindsight.

Shortcuts

- In the long term, investments will deliver **better returns** than savings in cash. Remember the concept of evolution ultimately drives this and will allow companies to continually get better.

- Before starting to invest, it is vital to have **sufficient cash available** to meet short-term needs, including any emergencies.

This is the foundation which allows you to build you long term investments.

- If someone's financial goal is **more than five years away,** they should be investing.

- The **longer the term, the better the return,** even if there are major negative events along the way because 75% of the time markets go up and 25% of the time do they go down.

- Asset classes include **cash, stocks and shares (equities), bonds, property** and **commodities.**

- Investments in equities have a **75%** chance of **outperforming** cash savings over **5** years, a **95%** chance over **10** years and a **99%** chance over **15** years.

- Investments will **fall in value** at some point, accept this and if possible, buy more because over time they will go up more often than they will go down. Falls in the market are sale events.

- The further away people are in time from their financial goal, **the more risk** they can afford to take.

- You can **reduce the risk** by **diversifying** investments across a range of different **asset classes,** and by using skilled investment managers.

- Major **financial crashes** stick in people's minds and make them fearful, but markets always recover, often surprisingly quickly. By the time you feel better, markets are already up. This is because they are forward looking and generally reflect the expectation of what will be happening in 6 month's time.

- **High concentrations** in single Co shares or assets have shown me the most mistakes. At some point take risk off the table or set stop losses to avoid major fallbacks if things don't go to plan.

- When selling investments **avoid anchoring** to round numbers like £1.00 per share or when the valuation hits £100,000. Know your exit amount and realise gains that achieve your objectives.

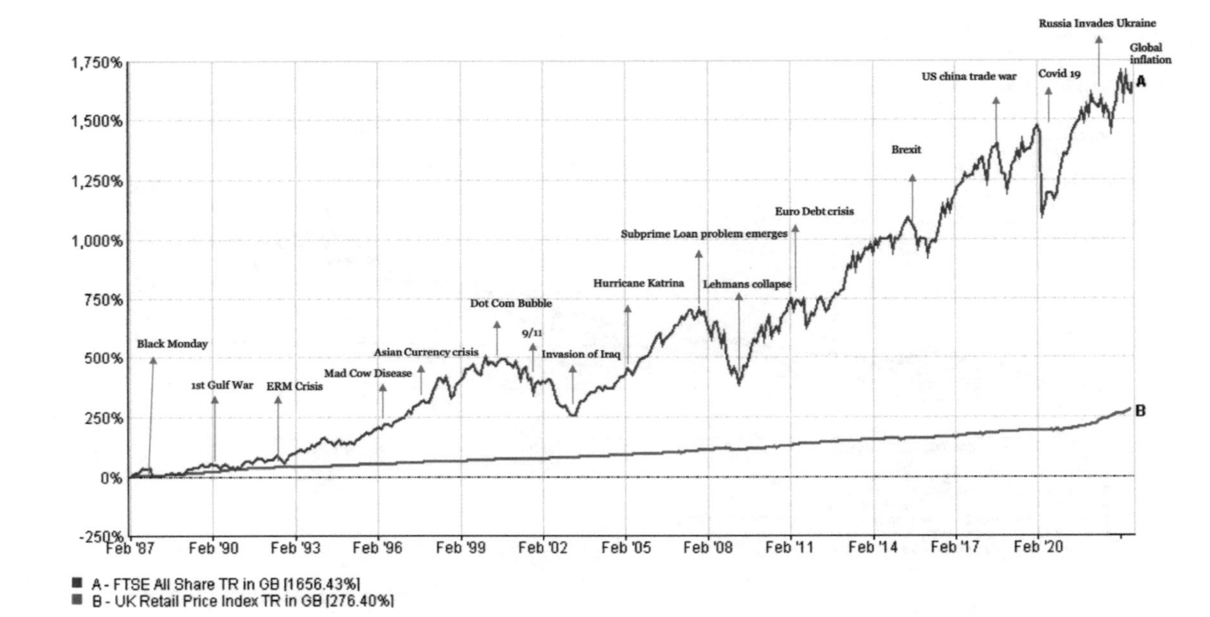

30/01/1987 - 21/07/2023 Data from FE fundinfo2023

Please be aware that past performance is not indicative of future performance, and the price of units and the income from them may go down as well as up. Equity based investments do not provide the same security and capital characteristics of bank or building society deposits.

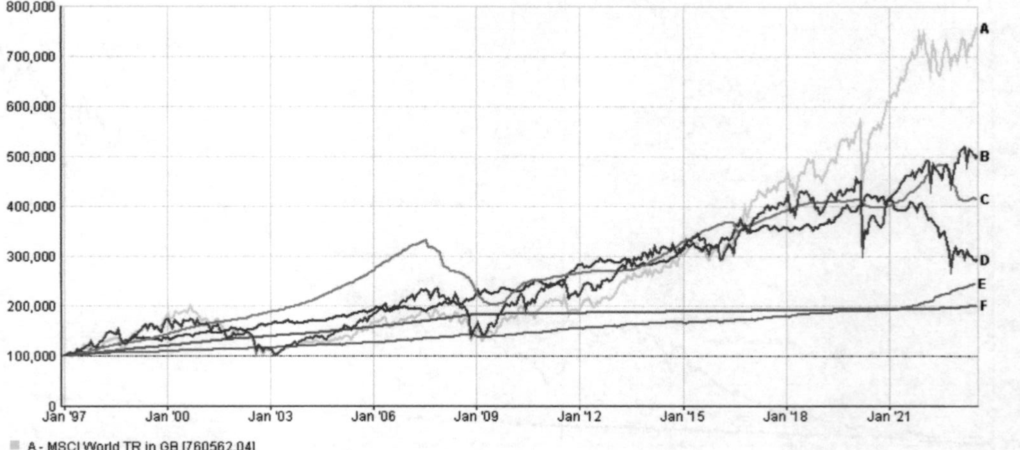

Please be aware that past performance is not indicative of future performance, and the price of units and the income from them may go down as well as up. Equity based investments do not provide the same security and capital characteristics of bank or building society deposits.

Diversification

Everything has its time in the sun.

No-one can predict which investment is going to produce the best returns year after year, but there are two things we can be sure of:

1. The best-performing investment in one year can often turn out to be the worst-performing investment the next year.
2. By spreading your money across a selection of asset types, countries and sectors, your investments stand a better chance of achieving more consistent returns.

Please be aware past performance is not indicative of future performance.

	CALENDAR YEAR										
RANK	2011	2012	2013	2014	2015	2016	2017	2018	2019	2020	2021
1st	UK Gilts	European Equities	US Equities	US Equities	UK Property	US Equities	Emerging Market Equities	UK Property	US Equities	Emerging Markets Equity	US Equities
2nd	UK Propert y	Emerging Market Equities	European Equities	UK Property	US Equities	Commodities	Far East Equities	UK Gilts	Emerging Markets Equity	US Equities	Commodities
3rd	US Equitie s	UK Equities	UK Equities	UK Gilts	Far East Equities	Emerging Market Equities	European Equities	Deposit A/c	European Equities	Far East Equities	UK Equities
4th	Deposit A/c	Far East Equities	Far East Equities	Far East Equities	European Equities	Far East Equities	UK Equiti es	US Equities	UK Equities	UK Gilts	European Equities
5th	UK Equities	US Equities	UK Property	Emerging Market Equities	UK Gilts	European Equities	US Equiti es	Commodities	Far East Equities	Deposit A/c	UK Property
6th	European Equities	UK Gilts	Deposit A/c	UK Equities	UK Equities	UK Equities	UK Prope rty	Far East Equities	Commodities	European Equities	Far East Equities
7th	Commoditi es	UK Property	Emerging Market Equities	Deposit A/c	Deposit A/c	UK Gilts	UK Gilts	European Equities	UK Gilts	UK Property	Deposit A/c
8th	Far East Equities	Deposit A/c	UK Gilts	European Equities	Emerging Market Equities	UK Property	Deposit A/c	UK Equities	UK Property	Commodities	UK Gilts
9th	Emerging Markets Equity	Commodities	Commodities	Commodities	Commodities	Deposit A/c	Commodities	Emerging Market Equities	Deposit A/c	UK Equities	Emerging Market Equities

FTSE All-Share
MSCI UK Quarterly Benchmark
FTSE British Government All Stocks
FTSE All-World Asia Pacific
FTSE All-World Europe
FTSE All-World North America
Moneyfacts Instant Access notice £10K
MSCI Emerging Markets Growth
Dow Jones-UBS Commodities

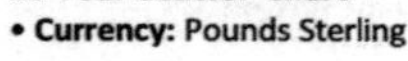

10 Year Scatter Chart

- **Currency:** Pounds Sterling

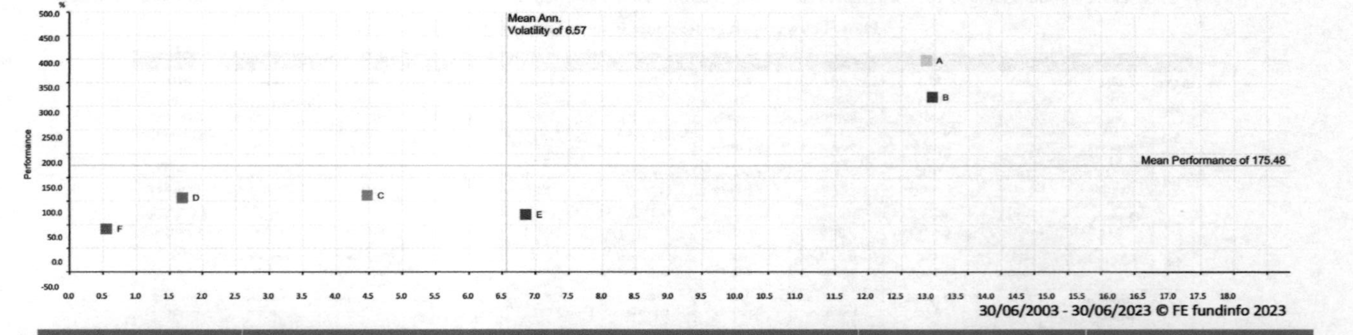

30/06/2003 - 30/06/2023 © FE fundinfo 2023

Key	Name	Performance	Volatility
A	MSCI World TR in GB	398.98	12.87
B	FTSE All Share TR in GB	320.84	12.96
C	FE UK Property Proxy TR in GB	111.97	4.47
D	UK Retail Price Index TR in GB	107.61	1.69
E	FTSE Actuaries UK Conventional Gilts All Stocks TR in GB	72.24	6.85
F	Bank Of England Base Rate TR in GB	41.24	0.55

The scatter chart and table illustrate the risk, represented by volatility, of the various assets, against return, represented by performance. The chart will return performance and volatility over 10 years to latest month end and in composite currency.
In this example it is form 30th June 2003 – 2023 and in pound sterling.

Please be aware that past performance is not indicative of future performance, and the price of units and the income from them may go down as well as up. Equity based investments do not provide the same security and capital characteristics of bank or building society deposits.

Chapter 9: Tax and Investment Wrappers

The tax system has a deserved reputation for being unnecessarily complicated but there are only three major taxes that people are likely to need to be familiar with at various stages in their lives: income tax, capital gains tax and inheritance tax. Please note, all taxes are always subject to change and regularly do change, as successive governments make their preferred changes to the tax system.

Income Tax

In early life, most people will pay little or no tax at all. They are likely to be either earning very little in an apprenticeship or a first job, or they might be studying and working only part-time. For individuals who are employees, tax is very straightforward because they will pay income tax, and perhaps National Insurance, through the Pay As You Earn (PAYE) system. There are different earnings thresholds and the more someone earns, the higher the rate of tax they pay. The first **£12,570** of income is tax-free; this is known as the **personal allowance.** Young people are allocated a **National Insurance** number from the age of 16, but they do not pay any National Insurance unless they earn over **£242 a week** (£12,584 p.a.).

In our twenties, we tend to start paying more income tax –

and to become more aware of it! After the £12,570 personal allowance, income between £12,571 and £50,270 per annum is taxed at the **basic rate** of **20%**. Earnings between £50,271 and £125,140 are taxed at the **higher rate** of **40%**. Earnings over £125,140 are taxed at the **additional rate** of **45%**.

Once someone earns **over £100,000**, they are subject to something called the **'tapering' of the personal allowance**. For every £2 earned over £100,000, £1 is lost from the personal allowance, so that your personal allowance becomes zero once you earn £125,140, creating an effective tax rate of 60%. It is possible to gain back lost personal allowance by making additional pension contributions, as we will see later in this chapter.

It is always popular to suggest that 'the wealthy' should pay more tax but, interestingly, the top 1% of earners already pay around 30% of all income tax and the top 10% pay 60% of all income tax in the UK.

There is a very specific order in which income is taxed. This is important because different income sources may be taxed at different rates, and the order may determine whether certain tax-free allowances are available or not. Earnings, pension income, rent and savings are taxed at the basic, higher and additional rates of 20%, 40% and 45% and dividends at 8.75%,

33.75% and 39.35%. Non-savings income is taxed first, then savings income (including offshore bond gains), followed by dividend income, and finally onshore bond gains. This order is sometimes represented as a pyramid diagram, starting at the bottom with non-savings income.

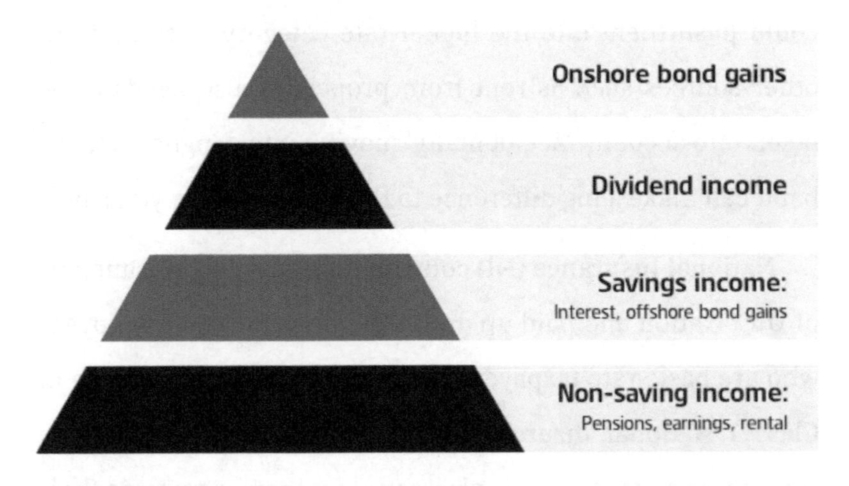

Onshore and offshore bonds are types of investment bond, which is a type of investment wrapper and we will talk more about them later in the chapter.

The simplest way to describe the different levels of income tax is to imagine filling up a measuring jug with water. The first amount that is poured in is tax-free. The next amount is taxed at the basic rate of 20%, then at the higher of 40%, and then at the additional rate of 45%.

The different income tax bands are also used to determine the level of tax-free interest on savings. A non-taxpayer or a basic rate taxpayer will get the first £1,000 in interest tax-free; for a higher rate taxpayer, it is £500; then for additional rate taxpayers, it is zero. Non taxpayers can also receive an additional £5,000 savings allowance on top of the initial amount. People need to be aware they might have interest from savings that could push them into the higher-rate category. Income from other sources such as rent from properties also needs to be taken into account. 'Accidentally' moving into a higher rate tax band can make a big difference to the amount of tax you pay.

National Insurance (NI) contributions are a significant part of UK taxation and paid up until state pension age. Employees who are basic-rate taxpayers pay 12% of their taxed income in Class 1 National Insurance contributions, deducted directly from their pay (employers also pay a percentage towards their employees' National Insurance, currently 13.8%). Once someone becomes a higher rate taxpayer, their National Insurance contributions drop to 2% of their earnings above this threshold.

If an employee earns above the lower earnings limit (£123 per week or £6,396 p.a., the amount at which you get a NI stamp) and below the primary threshold (£242 per week or £12,584 p.a.), they will not have to pay contributions, but their National Insurance record will be 'credited', which counts towards the state pension and some other contributary state benefits.

Self-employed people must pay Class 4 national insurance contributions if their profits are more than £12,570 a year. They also need to pay a flat rate of Class 2 national insurance contributions of £3.15 per week (£163.80 pa) to get their state pension stamp. They pay 9% for earnings in the basic rate band and the same 2% above higher rate tax band.

Capital gains tax

Capital gains tax (CGT) is a tax on the profit made when selling an asset if it has increased in value at the time of being sold. CGT is payable on gains from the sale of **personal possessions worth £6,000** or more - things like **jewellery, paintings, antiques, coins and stamps**, or **valuable sets** of things, such as vases. One of the most common assets that are liable for CGT when profits are realised are single company **shares, equity funds in unit trusts, property and corporate bonds.**

Cars for personal use and **possessions with a lifespan of less than 50 years** (including antique clocks and watches) are **exempt** from CGT. Everyone's **main residence** is **exempt** from CGT, but gains from the sale of **any other property** - second homes or buy-to-lets – are **liable** to the tax.

A good capital gains tax calculator is available on the HMRC website to work out what tax is due.

CGT is only paid if any overall gains for the tax year are

more than the **annual exempt amount** (after any losses and reliefs). For most individuals in the UK, the **annual exempt amount is £6,000** (tax year 2023-24). Any profit above this is taxed at **10%** for basic-rate taxpayers and **20%** for higher-rate taxpayers. Higher rates of **18%** and **28%** respectively apply to profits arising from the sale of **residential property**.

Income from capital gains is treated as part of your income for the tax year in which the gains are made, which means that income tax bands are used to calculate how much CGT is owed, making things quite complicated. If someone earns £40,000 a year, for example, they are a basic-rate taxpayer because the income tax band does not change until the £50,270 threshold is reached. If they sold assets and achieved a profit of £20,000, the first £10,270 of that profit (the difference remaining from the basic-rate tax band) would be taxed at 10%. The remainder would be taxed at 20%, because their income in that tax year will now have crossed the £50,270 threshold. If the capital gains arose from the sale of property rather than from the sale of other assets, the tax rates would be 18% and 28%. The 8% surcharge on capital gains from residential property was introduced several years ago because the government felt that too many people were buying multiple properties, which meant fewer first time-buyers could get on the property ladder. This is intended to disincentivise people from buying second properties: the government introduces heavier taxes on things they do not want the population to consume, such as cigarettes and alcohol; second properties now fall into a similar category. The government uses classic 'nudge' mentality (named after the 2012 bestselling book Nudge by the behavioural scientist Richard Thaler) if they want to incentivize people to do or not do something. This is why pension contributions have good tax incentives: it is expensive for the government to fund people in later life and we are all living longer, so the government incentives us to build up our own pension funds.

When CGT is payable on residential property, it must be paid within 60 days. All other CGT is payable on 31 January the following tax year. If you do make a gain on the sale of assets other than property, keep that profit in a savings account, earn some interest on it, and then pay it to the government when it is due. Never pay it early!

The annual exempt amount for CGT fell to £6,000 in the tax year 2023-24 from its previous level of £12,300. It will be reduced to £3,000 in the tax year 2024-25. This means more and more people will need to declare capital gains and pay the tax.

The bigger the gain someone makes on anything, the more reluctant they can become to sell it because of CGT. They feel as if they are losing money, and this persuades some people to hang onto assets when they might be better off selling them. It is important to remember that CGT is a lower tax than many others, and we shouldn't let taxation prevent us from doing whatever is in our best interest at the time. However, it is also sensible to take whatever action we can to minimise our exposure to tax. If you have made a loss on an investment, for example, you are entitled to sell that investment at a loss and to carry forward those losses indefinitely via your tax return. It might be sensible at certain times to sell shares that have gone down in value and use the loss to offset other gains. Using a financial advisor to help you decide on the timing of the disposal of assets is always a good idea.

Gifts to spouses or civil partners are not subject to CGT, and using spousal benefits in this way is very useful. A married person can gift assets to their spouse to make best use of both their individual allowances. Imagine a couple made up of a higher-rate taxpayer and a basic-rate taxpayer. The higher-rate taxpayer could gift assets, shares or property (or a percentage ownership of a property) to their spouse, and the spouse could then sell the asset in their name. Remember, as we saw earlier, that the capital gain may push the spouse into a higher tax bracket for that particular tax year. It will always be worth moving some of the gain into the name of the lower tax-rate payer, but only the portion of the gain that stays within the tax threshold will be taxable at the lower rate of tax; the rest of the gain will be taxed at the higher rate.

CGT is not paid on anything that is given to **charity**. Let's say someone has bought something for £5,000 and it has increased in value to £10,000. They do not necessarily want to pay the tax so they could gift it to charity. If they do the latter, they can also claim basic rate income tax relief via **Gift Aid** (**20%** or **25%** for additional rate taxpayers), increasing the value of their gift. If this is declared on a person's tax return, then they can also reduce their own tax if they are a higher rate taxpayer or above as they can claim back the additional 20% or 25% tax on the gift.

People who sell business they have built up, or shares in a business, can claim **Business Asset Disposal Relief.** Qualifying businesses benefit from a 10% tax rate on the first £1 million gain from the sale of the business. Anything over £1 million is charged at 20%. This was previously known as 'Entrepreneur's Relief' and the aim, of course, was to encourage people to start new enterprises and grow the economy.

Inheritance tax

As people get older, it is wise to begin thinking about **inheritance tax (IHT)**. The first **£325,000** of an estate is **tax-free** (this is called the nil rate band or the basic threshold). People who are **gifting their main residence** down their bloodline to children, adopted **children** or stepchildren have an extra **£175,000 tax-**

free (the residence nil rate band). People who do not have children and gift their house to siblings or their nephew or niece do not qualify under this rule.

Widows and widowers **inherit** their deceased spouse's **nil rate bands.** Typically, on death, most people give all their assets to their spouse to make sure they are provided for. This would mean the whole of their nil rate band is unused, so when the second partner dies, their basic threshold becomes **£650,000.** That is in addition to the £175,000 allowance where the estate is being gifted to children, which is also inherited when a spouse dies. This is why there is the common rule of thumb that **£1 million is exempt from IHT**, because someone who has inherited their spouse's allowances will have **£650,000** in basic threshold allowance and **£350,000** in allowances for gifting their residence to their children. If someone has a main residence worth less than the residence nil rate band – say £250,000 – then they would only have a residence nil rate band which is equal to the value of that property, in this example £250,000. The standard rate of IHT on the value of estate in excess of the various allowances is **40%.**

If someone has over **£2 million** in assets, for every £2 over £2 million, they lose £1 of the resident's nil rate band. People who own multiple properties can quite easily fall into this category and their estates can be hit quite hard on the second death.

It is important to consider ways to reduce the IHT burden by taking advantage of various tax allowances. Everyone can **give a total of £3,000** away during the tax year to one or more people, exempt from IHT. They can also give a tax-free gift for a **wedding or civil partnership of up to £5,000** for a child, up to **£2,500** for a grandchild or great-grandchild and up to **£1,000** to anyone else. It is essential to **make a record** all such gifts.

There is also the **small gift allowance** where people can give **£250** per person to anyone as many times as they want during the year. Not many people do this as they amount to quite trivial sums and each one needs to be recorded. Gifts for Christmas or birthdays given from ordinary income are exempt from IHT.

Another important allowance is the '**normal expenditure out of income**' rule. If someone has £50,000 income from a pension, dividends or rentals and they can demonstrate that they only need £25,000 to cover their typical outgoings, they are allowed to give away the remaining £25,000 tax-free because it does not affect their standard of living – the money is a gift from excess income. However, the word 'normal' (as in 'normal expenditure') is essential from the taxman's perspective: it must be possible to show that you regularly give such money to your extended family. Making regular payments towards annual holidays for the family would count, for example, as would regular payments to help with the cost of school or university fees. Making a one-off payment to help with some home improvements would be unlikely to qualify, unless you could show a pattern of such contributions and be able to argue that you regularly make payments to help with a family member's home maintenance and improvement. Keeping good records of all such expenditures is essential, because HMRC will want documentation. Getting professional advice is highly recommended.

Most people worry about the **seven-year rule** for gifts. When someone gives something away, it is technically still part of their estate. If they die within seven years, it comes back into their estate as if they never gave it away. It's important to note that if this gift still amounts to less than the nil rate band then it's tax free, but if it is over the individuals nil rate band then IHT becomes payable.

Let's say someone gifts £100,000 and the IHT band has been fully used up. If they die within three years, then it is taxed at **40%**. If they die between three and seven years after the gift was made, the amount is taxed on a sliding scale called '**tapering relief**' and the tax reduces by 20% each year after the third anniversary of the gift: three to four years after death, **32%**; four to five years, **24%**; five to six years, **16%**; six to seven years, **8%**; and seven years, **0%**. Tapering relief is only applied if the total value of gifts made in the seven years before death **exceeds the tax-free threshold.**

Many people are reluctant to gift money until they know they will not need it, for example, for care costs. But taxes on inheritance are only paid upon death and nobody knows exactly when they will die. The cost can be considerable because once someone is over the nil rate threshold, everything is taxed at 40%: a very high level. Thinking ahead about IHT liabilities and allowances and doing some tax planning can make a big difference; the government can be the main beneficiary if people are not careful. inheritance tax planning is quite technical, so professional advice is recommended.

The more we can plan around all of our taxes, the better. People can choose when to pay CGT, for example, to some extent, by selecting when they dispose of assets, giving them a greater level of control and the opportunity to set losses against gains. If someone holds onto an asset until they die, there is no CGT to pay on it at death, but then IHT kicks in on the value of the estate above the nil rate band, at the rate of 40% as opposed to CGT at 20%. Planning is everything.

ISAs and pensions

To help people reduce their tax liability, we always point them first towards ISAs and pensions because they are the most tax-efficient investments – what financial advisors call 'no-brainers'. All funds grow tax free while inside these wrappers and so offer some of the highest tax efficiency available to an investor.

ISAs are incredibly useful because the money can normally be accessed at any time and money kept in an ISA is protected from tax forever. This means we don't have to make as high a rate of return on the money to end up with the same total return in real terms.

ISAs are completely exempt from both income tax and CGT but not inheritance tax. As we saw in an earlier chapter, everyone has a **£20,000 ISA allowance** per person every tax year, so a typical couple can protect a total of **£40,000** p.a. in ISAs every year. **Junior ISAs** can be opened for children for a total of **£9,000** a year. The money is locked in until a child reaches the age of 18, at which point the Junior ISA becomes an ordinary cash ISA, though children can begin to manage a junior ISA account from the age of 16. Children born between 1 September 2002 and 2 January 2011 may have a **Child Trust Fund** that could be paid into a Junior ISA.

With **pensions**, there is an **annual allowance of £60,000** per year per person from April 2023 (increased from £40,000 in tax year 2022-23). This is the amount someone can pay into a pension pot before having to pay tax on those contributions. The money is treated, in effect, as if you had not earned it. If someone is a higher-rate taxpayer, for example, they will get 40% **income tax relief** on their pension contributions. There is no other investment I know of that gives a 40% return on day one and putting money into a pension fund is incredibly tax efficient. Pensions are also exempt from IHT. Many people now are holding on to their pension funds and spending other monies down to preserve them so they can then pass them on to the next generation.

If a person dies **before the age of 75**, the whole of their pension fund is **tax free.** If someone dies after 75, their pension fund is **free of IHT**, but withdrawals are treated as income and so **income tax** is charged on anything that is drawn down, just as it is on all normal income. A pension can be passed on through the generations, paying out to children, grandchildren, and their children. In this way, pensions can be like a **family trust** for many people.

Where people choose to spend down their pension pots in their own lifetime, **25%** is **tax-free** on sums up to the **lifetime allowance** (£1,073,100 for the tax year 2023-24). The rest is subject to **income tax.**

As we said earlier, when we buy our groceries, some things go in the fruit bowl, some in the fridge, and some in the freezer. Pensions represent assets in the freezer: money that is not needed for a long period, or until someone is at least 55 (57 from 2028).

Other Investment wrappers

Pensions and ISAs are the two most obvious and simplest ways of reducing tax liabilities and should be everyone's first port of call. Additional **Investment wrappers** offer a third option for money in excess of the ISA and pension allowances that someone wants to invest. These offer different tax exposure and so provide diverse planning opportunities for clients. Investment wrappers include **unit trusts** and **open-ended investment companies (OEICs).**

Unit trusts provide **dividends and interest** from shares, equity or bond funds held which are subject to income tax, as we discussed in the earlier chapter on Investment. There is a £1,000 dividend allowance in the 2023-24 tax year, dropping to £500 the year afterwards and the savings nil rate band can be useful to keep more returns tax free. These bands are all open to change and they will of course evolve. CGT is also payable on capital growth realized on sale or when switching unit trust funds but, as before, it is possible to some extent to control how much tax is paid and when. Often someone can lock in gains each year by switching funds and then using their CGT allowance to set a new base cost of that investment which won't be taxable or may sell a proportion of their investment and move £20,000 each year into their ISA. This allows someone to tax efficiently move more money each year into their tax-free holdings without having to find new money to invest.

Investment bonds are designed to deliver medium to long term capital growth. Investors pay a lump sum to an insurance company and the money is invested, usually across a range of funds. There is an element of life insurance, and on death the bond will typically pay out slightly more than the value of the fund - perhaps 1% more. Gains on investment bonds are liable to income tax when withdrawals are made, but it is possible to take what is called a tax deferred withdrawal out of bonds so that, for example, someone could put £100,000 into an investment bond and take up to 5% per annum of their original capital without paying any tax on it. The money can be withdrawn monthly, if required. It's a bit like saying, "I'm going to just take out some of my original capital and leave the profits to run." Investment bonds offer another way to control your taxation. Investment bonds can be gifted into a trust or given away for IHT purposes.

Fund switches within the fund do not incur CGT and asset incomes do not incur income tax on an individual, so the annual reporting and maintenance for investors is low. There is also a benefit called 'top slicing relief' which can reduce higher rate tax on what is called a **chargeable event** by allowing the bondholder to spread the investment gains over the number of years the bond has been held. It is available to non-taxpayers, starting rate taxpayers or basic rate taxpayers who, after adding chargeable event gains to their income, become higher rate taxpayers. These wrappers tend to offer the most benefit to those individuals who are higher or additional rate taxpayers and intend to access the money later in life when they become lower rate taxpayers (typically retired) or want to gift these monies to lower tax paying family members.

We talked in the chapter on Investment about **AIM** shares (formerly the 'alternative investment market') where investments are made in smaller businesses. They are far more volatile than most other shares, so returns can be quite spectacular – for good and bad! Most AIM stocks are **exempt from IHT** if they have been held for more than two years.

Additional wrappers offering income tax relief include **enterprise investment schemes (EISs)** and **venture capital trusts (VCTs)**. These can be attractive to additional-rate taxpayers who are happy to take some risks with growth businesses in the UK. Investments in these two wrappers are eligible for **30% tax relief.** VCT's offer both tax free growth and dividends while EIS also offers growth **free from CGT** but has the additional benefit of being **exempt from IHT** if held for 2 years or more. This tax relief is an incentive from the government to create growth in the economy – the investments are in small growth businesses with the potential to become the bigger employers of tomorrow, stimulating the economy and generating tax revenues for the government. Typically for every £1 the government gives in tax relief in this way they receive back £4 in the form of new income tax, NI and CGT receipts from these growing businesses. VCTs and EISs are higher-risk investments so people should always take advice before investing and consider the wider aspects of planning that are unique to these types of investment.

There are other wrappers that invest in **unlisted businesses and corporate debt** that are also IHT free. Investment houses create these companies and invest in things like wind farms and renewable energy, or secure debt for corporates at very low loan-to-value ratios. They are designed to be relatively low risk and, as a result, offer limited returns, but they are **not subject to IHT** if the shares are held for **two years** or more. They can be useful for older investors to shelter money from IHT. They are also used by younger entrepreneurs who may make large profits from the sale of their businesses and use these wrappers to shelter some of the profits from taxation. As long as someone has held those kinds of investments for two of the previous five years, they remain exempt from IHT.

ISAs, pensions and investment wrappers can be seen as 'oven-ready' ways of tax planning that remove a lot of the strain and help individuals build up wealth or achieve other financial goals, depending upon the stage in life they have reached. A financial advisor can be especially useful in this context, acting almost as a chef, adding an ingredient here and there and blending things to give the investor the ideal result for their circumstances. Advisors will also carry out essential reviews of investment portfolios to ensure that they are still best suited to investors' needs at different points in their life.

Shortcuts

- There are three main taxes that people need to plan for: **income tax, capital gains tax (CGT) and inheritance tax (IHT).** Understand the rates that apply to you and when you have to pay them.

- **ISAs** and **pensions** are the most **tax-efficient** forms of investment. These are 'no brainers', especially for higher-rate taxpayers. Maximise tax efficiently and by default you don't need to take as much risk because there is limited tax drag on compounding gains.

- **Gifts** to spouses, civil partners or charities are **not subject to CGT**. Consider these each year.

- People who **inherit their spouse's IHT allowances** on death and who leave their property to their children can leave assets, including the property, worth **£1 million** without incurring IHT.

- People can use their **annual exemption, small gift allowances** and their **normal expenditure out of income** allowance to **reduce IHT**.

- Inheritance tax planning is complicated so **professional advice** should be sought and **gifts** of money or assets or the **sale of assets** before a persons' death should be carefully **documented.** This is an ever-evolving area, start small if needed and build up year on year as you get older and have a higher conviction on how much of your wealth you need to retain.

- **Tax wrappers** other than ISAs and pensions are incredibly useful once those two allowances are utilised. These include **unit trusts, OEICs, investment bonds, enterprise investment schemes (EIS)** and **venture capital trusts (VCT)** which offer many advantages, especially the benefit of wrapper diversification.

- The most suitable and tax-efficient investments for individuals change depending on the **stage in life** they have reached.

- Getting the **timing** right and **fulfilling the criteria** exactly is important for many investments and wrappers designed to protect money from tax offer greater flexibility when the time comes when you want to spend the money.

- Avoid becoming obsessed with tax planning to the expense of liquidity of assets, time and spending.

In 2022/23, UK government revenues – or public sector current receipts – were £1,017 billion, equivalent to 40% of GDP.[1]

Aside from taxes and duties, the government also receives other receipts, largely from income generated by public corporations – such as through social housing– and from interest payments on its assets, such as student loans.

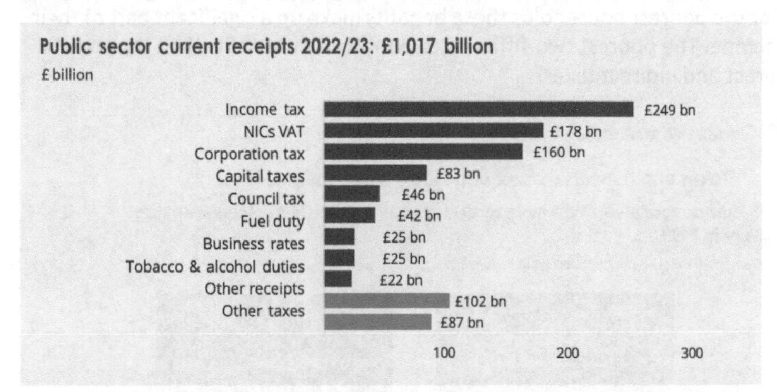

Notes: Capital taxes include stamp duties, capital gains tax and inheritance tax. Corporation tax here includes the energy profits levy (EPL). We exclude the EPL elsewhere.
Source: ONS. Public sector current receipts: Appendix D

Data for 2022/23 are sourced from ONS's Public sector finances, UK: April 2023 (published 23 May 2023). Figures may be revised in subsequent publications

Overall tax and benefit system

The overall tax and benefit system is redistributive.

Household incomes described above include cash benefits from government. For the poorest households these benefits make up a significant part of their income. The poorest two-fifths receive more cash benefits than they pay in direct and indirect taxes.

IFS, The effect of taxes and benefits on UK inequality, 2019

Taxes and benefits as % of disposable income, 2020/21

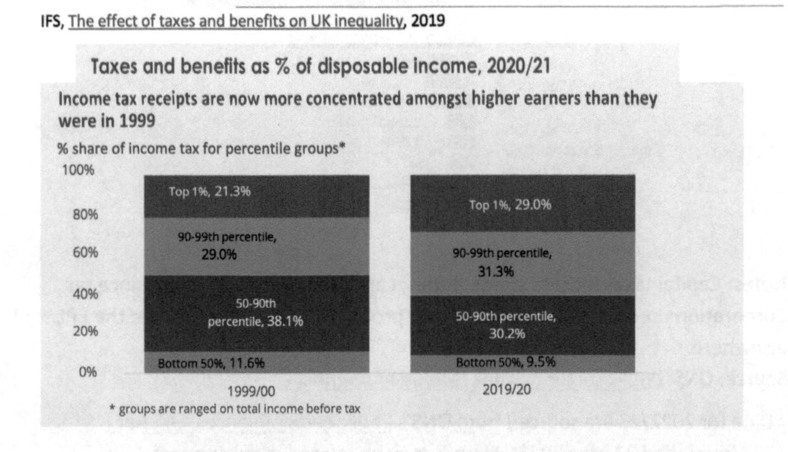

Source: HMRC. Table 2.4 Shares of total Income Tax Liability

International comparisons

The UK raises slightly less tax revenues, as a share of GDP, than the average of countries in the Organisation for Economic Co-operation and Development (OECD). In 2021, OECD countries' tax revenues were equivalent to 34.1% of GDP; in the UK they were 33.5% of GDP.

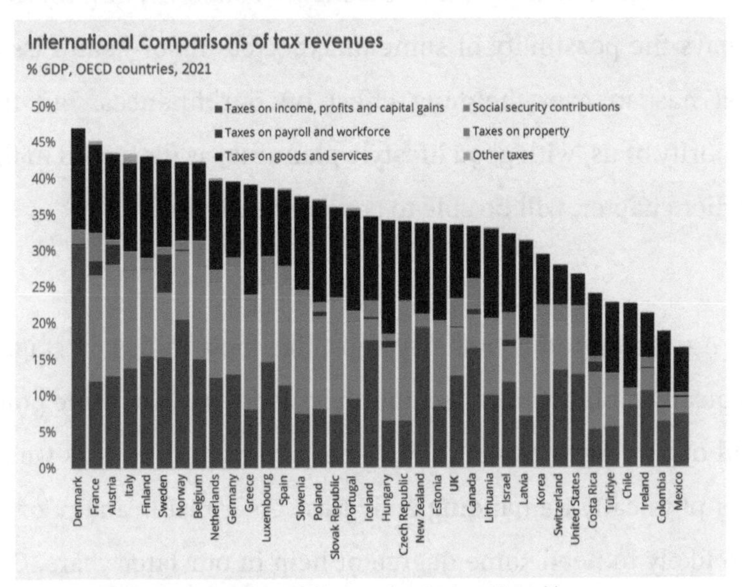

Source: OECD. Revenue statistics - OECD countries: Comparative tables

In 2021, the UK raised more from taxes on property, as a share of GDP, than all but 4 of 36 OECD countries for which complete data are available. 14 countries raised more from taxes on income, profits and capital gains than the UK, while 21 raised less.[48]

48 Complete data are available for 36 OECD countries in 2021

Chapter 10: Care in Older Age

One of the most common issues people have is an understandable concern about the possible costs of being looked after in older age if we can no longer look after ourselves, but for most of us this can be covered by our normal financial planning. I don't want to play down people's reasonable concerns, and there is always the possibility of some unexpected major health issue that has an overwhelming effect on our finances, but the majority of us, with good **lifestyle planning**, as discussed in the earlier chapter, will be able to cope perfectly well.

Ageing is gradual and develops, like most things, in stages. Typically mobility may become an issue for us all at some point and our strength can tend to wane in our later years as we do less physically demanding activities. As a result, many of us are likely to need some degree of help in our later years. Our families may not be living nearby, or they may be unable to fit regular care into their busy lives. Just as many people employ gardeners and builders to help us with things we don't have the time or skills to do ourselves in our earlier lives, so, as we get older, we may need help with day-to-day living. We may have mobility or strength issues or become more forgetful, and we may need help getting washed and dressed, preparing our meals and getting ourselves to bed.

The cost of such **domiciliary care** varies from region to region but it is currently in the range of **£15-£30 per hour**. If you needed two hours of care per day seven days a week, for example, at a rate of £20 ph., that would amount to **£14,560** per year.[9] Families will help as much as possible at this stage but it's not always practical to provide assistance all year round. Many local charities help with this so it's well worth looking around for support and assistance.

But for most of us, our outgoings go down as we get older – perhaps especially once we reach the age of 75. We tend to spend less on holidays, travel, outings, clothing and food. Typically, our **discretionary spend drops by a third**, and the cost of domiciliary care can often be absorbed by our typical previous spending levels. Domiciliary care, if needed, should be seen as a kind of **routine expense** that suits this stage of our lives. Food delivery is much easier to come by nowadays, and UberEats and Deliveroo can replace 'meals on wheels' in cities, though it can be much more difficult in rural locations to source the same level of support and is often more expensive.

If you have a physical or mental disability and have reached the state pension age, you should be eligible for **attendance allowance**. This is currently set at £68.10 per week if you need care in the day or night and £101.75 if you need care both day and night. Attendance allowance is **not means tested**, so it is

[9] HOW MUCH DOES IN HOME CARE COST In May 2023 - A Definitive Guide (ukcareguide.co.uk)

not affected by your savings or the value of your property. It is also not taxed. If you are under the state pension age but need help with daily activities because of long-term illness or disability, you may be eligible for the same allowances in the form of the **daily living component** of **Personal Independence Payment (PIP)**. You may also be able to claim the **mobility component** of PIP; this can be claimed on its own or in addition to the daily living component.[10]

The benefit system is quite complex, and people can be unaware of benefits they can claim. Fortunately, several age-related charities are available that offer excellent help and advice as well as the citizens advice bureau. The amounts of money involved are very unlikely to be enough to meet your needs, unfortunately, but it is important to claim any benefits you are entitled to: you've earned them!

An alternative to living in your own home with varying levels of domiciliary care is to move into sheltered or assisted housing. **Sheltered housing** offers a level of permanent staff in the form of a warden or other staff and has communal areas where people can socialise with their neighbours. There is typically a **24-hour emergency system** bringing immediate help, which is reassuring for people who are worried about some kind of emergency, such as a fall or a medical emergency. **Assisted housing** offers further levels of assistance, from

[10] What is Attendance Allowance? | Age UK

cleaning and shopping to various levels of personal and medical care, and also offers round-the-clock emergency assistance. Sheltered or assisted homes can be **rented or bought**, typically with a leasehold. If you sell your own home before moving into sheltered or assisted housing, this is likely to be an effective downsize, freeing up some of the capital in your home. Costs vary as ever, by region, and also on the level of care required, but a guide range for rental costs and care might be from **£15,000 to £20,000** per year.

Where a more significant level of care is needed, there is the option of **residential** or **nursing care.** Both offer comprehensive levels of personal care. Nursing care, as the name suggests, offers additional nursing facilities and medical assistance. These are the most expensive options and costs are likely to be in the region of **£27,000 to £39,000** per year for residential care and **£35,000 to £55,000** per year for nursing care.[11] Top of the range facilities in expensive parts of the country might cost as much as **£100,000** per year. I have known people who have moved overseas for their last few years or decided to spend it all on cruises as the medical care can be incredibly good. Costs can be a lot lower and the climate perhaps more agreeable, but there are risks associated with this approach and it must be considered carefully.

It is important to remember that most people only need to

[11] CARE HOME COSTS & CARE FEES | May 2023 (ukcareguide.co.uk)

move into residential or nursing care when they need full-time care near the end of their lives. We advise people to budget, if possible, for **five years** of residential care if they want complete peace of mind, but the average stay is more like **18 months.**

Another option for long-term care is to have a **live-in carer** in your own home, providing 24-hour care. This is expensive, since you are effectively paying for a professional carer, possibly with the specialist training needed to be able to carry out certain medical tasks, 24 hours a day 52 weeks of the year. One estimate of the average cost in the UK is £700-800 per week **(£36,400-£41,600 pa).** The cost is likely to almost double where two people in the house need care.[12] The cost also varies dramatically in relation to postcode, with the South East being particularly expensive compared to treatment in the North of the UK. It's not always practical but there are options to move to a different area to access better care at the same or even lower cost.

Local councils will **contribute to the cost of care,** but this is **means tested.** In England and Northern Island, anyone with assets of more than **£23,250** – the **'upper capital limit'** (UCL) – at the time of writing will not be eligible for funding from their local council towards the cost of care and will be required to **self-fund** their care. People with assets of between £14,250 and £23,250 will be asked to contribute to the cost on a sliding scale.

[12] LIVE IN CARER | What Is Live In Care & Its Cost? | May 2023 (ukcareguide.co.uk)

Anyone with assets of less than **£14,250** (the **'lower capital limit'** (LCL) – will have to pay from their income towards the cost of care, but the council will pay the remaining cost, leaving the person with money for personal expenses. If the reason for residential care is for certain medical reasons, then the NHS will cover the cost of care in an NHS care home. This is not always a certainty and often the local council, family members and the NHS will all be involved in making the final decision around what is the best option at this time.

The value of your **property** is **not taken into account** in council means tests **if you are still living there** and hope to return after a spell in care. It is also not included if your **spouse or partner lives in the property**, or in some other special circumstances – for example, if a close relative who is over 60 years of age or is incapacitated lives there. If you move **permanently** into residential or nursing care, the **value of your home will be included as capital** for the purposes of the means test. This may also be the case at any time once you have been in care for **more than 12 weeks.**[13] If you are eligible for council assistance, councils operate a **12-week disregard**, during which period they will 'disregard' the value of your property to give people time to decide whether to sell their house or not.

It is possible to ask your local council for a **deferred payment agreement** if your assets are low but the value of your property

[13] Property and paying for residential care (ageuk.org.uk)

would take you over the threshold for council support. If the council agrees, you will then pay what you can afford towards the cost of your care and the council will make up the difference and will defer repayment of their contribution until your property has been sold, which can be before or after your death. The council will take a legal charge on your property and will typically only lend 70-80% of the value of your home.

Councils will put a limit on the cost of care they are prepared to fund, so if a person wants to go to a more expensive care home, they will need to find the additional money themselves or ask a family member for financial help. If you can personally afford it, then go for it 100%. Seek out the very best care so you can be as comfortable as possible.

If anyone is judged to have deliberately got rid of assets by selling them or giving them away in order to qualify for council support for care, this may be disqualified under **deprivation of capital rulings**, and the value of the assets will still be taken into account in the means test. Deliberate **deprivation of income** is treated in the same way – if, for example, someone gave away or sold their rights to income from an occupational pension to qualify for council funding.

New legislation is expected to take effect as of October 2025, which will limit people's total liability for care costs over their lifetime. The legislation was originally intended to be introduced in October 2023, but has been delayed. The new rules will put a **cap of £86,000** on the amount anyone must pay for care in their lifetime. The capital limits mentioned above for assessing eligibility for local authority support will also rise to **£100,000** for the upper limit and **£20,000** for the lower limit. Care in your own home and residential care are both included in the £86,000 cap, but to level the playing field between home care and residential care, daily living costs in residential care – an amount calculated to cover rent, food and utility bills etc. – will not count towards the £86,000 cap and must continue to be paid once the cap is reached for charges other than daily living costs. Since the government has already postponed its proposal to introduce this measure in 2023, it cannot be taken for granted that the legislation will definitely come into force in 2025.

People who have what is classified as a 'primary health need' will have their ongoing healthcare funded by the NHS under what is known as **NHS continuing health care** (NHS CHC). There is, unfortunately, an ongoing debate about what qualifies as a primary health need and whether, for example, various forms of dementia should be included.

As discussed, many people **sell their home** when they move to sheltered, assisted housing or residential as the home is no longer needed and the cost of upkeep stops. This typically frees up capital that can be **drawn down** to pay for care costs or could be used to buy a **lifetime care plan**, where a lump sum is paid to an insurer who will then make regular payments towards the cost of care for the rest of one's life. The amount may not cover all of the costs of care, but in combination with any existing income in the form of pensions, annuities etc, it can make the necessary difference and provides peace of mind that such payments will be made for the rest of one's life, however long you may live. The money is paid directly to the care provider and is tax free, so it lasts much longer. There is the possibility, of course, that you will receive less in payments than the amount initially paid as a lump sum premium, depending on how long you live after buying the policy. However, it is possible to get annuity guarantee periods, typically of 5 or 10 years, so that if you have a 10-year guarantee on your policy, for example, and you die after 6 years, your beneficiaries will continue to receive payments for 4 years after your death. It is also possible to take out a joint annuity, which will continue to pay a spouse or partner until their own death after the death of the first partner. It is possible to claim the **attendance allowance** that we talked about earlier while you are in residential care to further contribute to overall costs; there may also be other benefits to which you are entitled. Not all people sell their property, and some family members may decide to rent the property out for a period to cover fees in the medium term. The time and effort of doing this along with managing tax returns and the emotional stress of care can be harder than many expect. It can be worth seeking professional help from letting agents and accountants at this time to make life easier.

Two final points are worth mentioning. It is never too early to set up a **lasting power of attorney (LPA)**, or to **make your will.**

Many people assume their **spouse will automatically be able to take over their financial affairs, but spouses and partners do not automatically have the power to take over your bank and pension accounts** or make decisions about your ongoing **healthcare.** To set up a lasting power of attorney, you need to apply to the **Court of Protection.** You can set up an LPA for an attorney to handle your property and financial affairs or your health and welfare issue, or both. You can appoint **more than one attorney.** They must be over the age of 18 and can be your spouse or partner, a relative, a friend or a professional, such as a solicitor. It is normally a good idea to appoint an attorney in addition to your spouse or partner in case you both die at the same time – falling under the proverbial bus, for example. You must then decide whether attorneys can make decisions **'jointly and severally'** or **'jointly'**. If it is the latter, all attorneys must all agree on a course of action. This can lead to disputes, but it also means that there is a 'second opinion' about key decisions. Everyone's circumstances are different, so everyone must decide which option is best for them. If the attorneys can decide 'jointly and severally', any one attorney can decide on their own. This is your insurance for managing your affairs when you can't decide for yourself, so lay out clear instructions in your expression of wishes, which should be easy to interpret and carry out. Choose people as attorneys that you trust to follow your wishes and act accordingly.

Completing the forms to appoint a Power of Attorney is quite an admin-heavy process involving witnesses' signatures, and it is an extremely good idea to do this at your leisure when you are fit and well and not under the kind of stress that comes with ill health. Various services are also available that will help you with the process. A Power of Attorney stays in place until you ask to remove an attorney or end your lasting power of attorney, so there is no risk of one expiring once it is in place. It only comes into effect once you lose the capacity to make decisions yourself, so if this never happens then there is no risk to you. It is always a good idea to set one up.

If you lose mental capacity before you have put a lasting power of attorney in place, it can make life very difficult for your spouse or partner, who may not even be able to access cash from your bank accounts for daily needs. They will need to apply to the Court of Protection to be accepted as a '**deputy**.' This will be a relatively lengthy and stressful process by comparison so plan ahead.

In the same way that not having put a power of attorney in place in case you become incapable of managing your own affairs can greatly inconvenience your spouse or partner and your family, dying without having made a will (**dying 'intestate'**) means that your estate will be allocated under the **rules of intestacy** rather than according to your personal wishes. A spouse or civil partner will inherit the first £322,000 of an estate. Where the estate is worth more than £322,000, the spouse or partner will also inherit half of the amount in excess of £322,000, with the remainder divided between any surviving children. Grandchildren will only inherit if their parent has died before the intestate grandparent, or if their parent inherits but dies before the age of 18 without having married or formed a civil partnership.[14] These dispositions may be very different from the ones you would have chosen yourself if you had written a will. The next chapter will look at the process of making a Will in more detail.

Shortcuts

- People are understandably worried about the potential cost of care as they get older and may find it harder to look after

[14] Who can inherit if there is no will – the rules of intestacy - Citizens Advice

themselves, but the cost can usually be covered with good **lifestyle planning.** Plan ahead so you know what to do and how to access the funds you need before you need it.

- **Domiciliary care** – carers who visit you at home to help with aspects of daily living – is readily available and should be seen as a routine expense of this stage of our life when our health and strength begins to fail.

- **Discretionary spending** tends to **fall by a third** as we get older (typically form 75 onwards) and can be used to **fund care at home.**

- **Sheltered** and **assisted housing** offer varying levels of care and routine assistance and **24-hour emergency help.**

- Moving into sheltered or assisted accommodation is likely to represent a **downsize** that **frees up capital** in your home to help pay for ongoing care costs.

- **Residential** or **nursing care** is **expensive**, but most people need such care for a relatively short period: **18 months** on average.

- Many people sell their home when they move into long-term care, freeing up capital, but it is unlikely that all of this capital will be needed to fund their care. The rest can be gifted, saved or invested to keep pace with inflation.

- **Live-in carers** who provide 24-hour care in your own

home are also expensive but can be a cheaper option than residential nursing care.

- Local councils offer support for long-term care, but this is **means tested.** Currently, anyone with assets worth more than **£23,250** is not eligible for any council support.

- The government plans to introduce an **£86,000 cap** on the amount anyone pays on care in their lifetime. The £23,250 threshold for assets above which people are not eligible for council support for care will also rise to **£100,000.**

Chapter 11: Making a Will

A Will is a legal document that allows you to state what you want to happen to your assets – your money, property, investments and possessions – when you die. In simple terms it is the actual record of what you want to happen at the end. If you do not have a Will in place, as we saw in the last chapter, then the courts will dispose of your assets following the laws of intestacy, which are set out in more detail in the flow chart at the end of this chapter. If you have children under the age of 18, it also allows you to stipulate who you want to look after them. Simply put, making a will clarifies your wishes and enables you to give your loved one's financial protection after you die.

There are different types of Will available to suit different needs. A basic Will for a single person is known as a **single Will** and is designed for people who want to record their own individual wishes. If your wishes are very similar to someone else's (typically your partner or spouse) then you may want to make what are called mirror Wills together. Mirror Wills typically name each partner as the main beneficiary of the other partner's estate, so that when the first partner dies, everything passes to the other partner. The Wills then typically sets out what money and/or possessions which beneficiaries should receive when the second partner dies, or if both partners die at the same time.

It is also possible to use a **trust Will** which creates a legal entity called a trust which is given control of some of your assets. **Trustees** are appointed to manage the trust according to the wishes of the person who created it. Trust Wills may be suitable if, for example, you want to provide for your partner but have children from a previous relationship; you can leave a sum of money for your partner and put money into the trust on behalf of the children. A trust Will can also be used to protect an inheritance if one of beneficiaries is unable to manage their finances: the trustees would manage their legacy on their behalf.

A trust Will can help to protect your estate against care home fees. If your partner dies and the house you live in is put into a trust, with you having a 'life interest' – the right to live in the house until you die or go into long term care – local authorities will only count your share of the house as being part of your assets, and not the share of the house that belongs to the trust. This is a complex area, but recent government rules suggest that putting a proportion of the property into a trust in this way would not be seen as the 'deliberate deprivation of assets' that we discussed earlier. It is worth noting that a trust Will must have been set up for you on the death of a partner. If you put your property into a trust in what is known as a **lifetime trust**, the house is likely to still be seen as your asset by local authorities when you are assessed for financial assistance if you go into care – they are likely to consider that putting the house into the trust is a 'deliberate deprivation of an asset'.[15]

I would always recommend that you speak to your **solicitor** or an expert **Will writing specialist**: the extremely cheap offers for Will writing that you may see advertised are likely to deliver at best an 'off the shelf' service and may not take your full circumstances sufficiently into account. A Will is a very important document, and it is very important that it is properly drawn up, both technically and in terms of ensuring your wishes are clearly expressed.

I would also recommend including as many of your more significant possessions as possible in your Will, as there can be disputes among beneficiaries about who should inherit a much-loved painting, for example, or an antique rug, and so on. I have heard of disputes between individual family members and the person appointed as executor of the Will, with family members arguing that they had always been promised they would inherit the painting, the rug or a piece of jewellery. Writing a comprehensive Will is the best way of avoiding these disputes. I am also in favour of discussing the contents of a Will with family members before you die, so that any disagreements can be aired

[15] Will trusts and lifetime trusts - Which?

and discussed while you are still alive. Some Wills create entirely unintentional discord in families which can be easily avoided if you can explain your intentions and reasoning while you are still alive. It is also possible that you have misunderstood something: you may have come to believe that one family member has greater needs than another and should get a bigger share of the inheritance – but this might not actually be the case.

You can make a Will at any time of your life. As I said in the previous chapter, it is highly recommended to make one quite early in life so that you have it in place if you die unexpectedly. You can always change the Will in later life if you want to make some adjustments. If you die intestate then things are more difficult for everyone, slower to deal with and involves a lot of time and bureaucracy. The intestacy chart on the next page highlights the added complexities, especially for people who are not married.

By making a Will you can:

- **Make life easier** for those dealing with your estate after death.

- Appoint people you trust ('**executors**') to carry out the terms of your will.

- Name the people or charities you want to benefit from your estate (‘**beneficiaries**’) and the proportions of your estate you want them to receive.

- Appoint people you trust (‘**guardians**’) to look after children under 18 years of age and make sure you have spoken to them about this responsibility before including it in the will.

- Leave gifts of specific items or fixed sums of money (‘**legacies**’)

- Create **trusts** to help protect your assets for future generations, protect against residential care costs or help vulnerable or disabled beneficiaries.

- State your **funeral** wishes.

- Everything can be easily changed at any time. It’s best to set up a will early and make small changes as life evolves.

- Avoid writing the will but not getting around to signing the forms and registering the will.

- Don’t overcomplicate things, make everything as fair and easy as possible to distribute to your beneficiaries.

Intestacy rules (English Law)

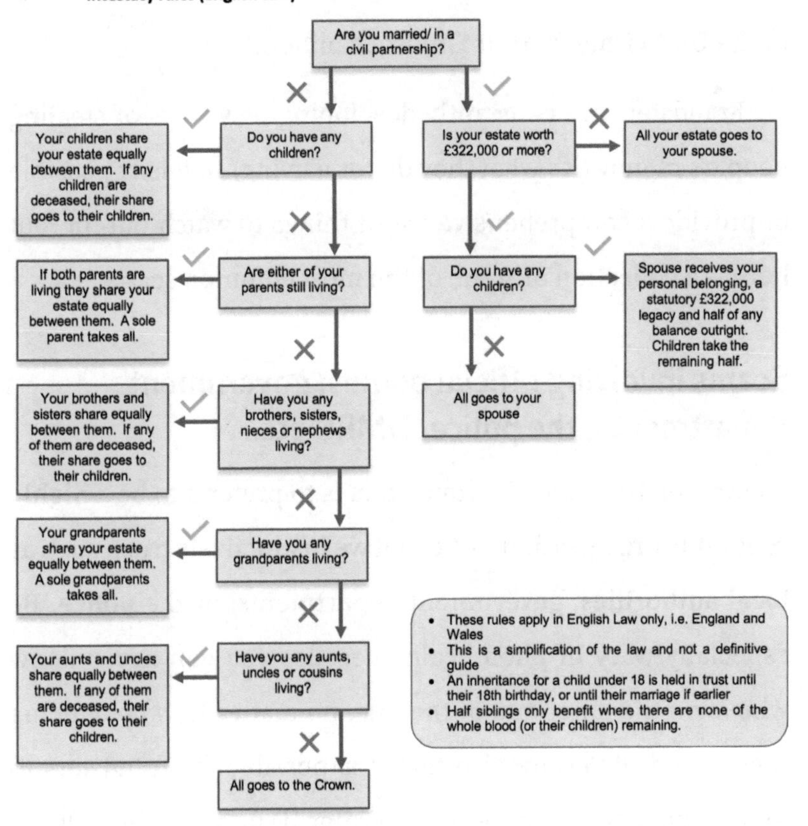

- These rules apply in English Law only, i.e. England and Wales
- This is a simplification of the law and not a definitive guide
- An inheritance for a child under 18 is held in trust until their 18th birthday, or until their marriage if earlier
- Half siblings only benefit where there are none of the whole blood (or their children) remaining.

Chapter 12: Fraud

This book is all about building wealth in order to have the lifestyle we want throughout our lives, so it is incredibly upsetting when I hear that people have lost money to fraudsters. A report by money.co.uk put the annual amount of money lost in the UK to fraudsters at almost £4 billion.[16]

Fraudsters are constantly developing new ways of stealing people's money (it's what they do for a living) so it isn't possible to provide a comprehensive list of things to watch out for, but here is a collection of some of the most common scams.

Scams involving official bodies, government departments, the police, HMRC etc.

A common trick used by fraudsters is to pretend to be a **highly reputable organisation** – one that we instinctively trust, such as **local authorities, government departments,** or the **police**. Be especially wary of phone calls, because you can never know who is on the other end of the line, no matter how convincing they sound. Be aware also that it is possible for fraudsters to 'spoof' real phone numbers: the Caller ID on your phone looks as if the call is coming from an organisation's genuine phone number, but it isn't. The same is true of email addresses. Sometimes they look entirely genuine but, in fact, have some small and easily overlooked spelling 'mistake' – a duplicated

[16] Quarterly Fraud and Cyber Crime Report 2023 | money.co.uk

letter, for example. Others look entirely plausible but don't really exist, for example secureemail@hmrc.gov.uk.

The recent cost of living crisis has produced a perfect example of fraudsters' ingenuity. People receive a phone call or some other form of communication purporting to be from their local authority, or the Department for Work and Pensions, or their energy provider, saying that they are eligible for a **cost-of-living payment**, but they need to collect your bank account details and other personal information in order to make the payment. The information can be used to take money directly from your account if you have been persuaded to give them enough details, or can be used for more indirect forms of identity fraud.

Messages might encourage victims to visit a **fake website** – it is very easy to create a website that looks very much like the real organisation's website – where they are asked to complete a form giving personal and bank account details. One message began "GOVUK: We have identified you as eligible for a discounted energy bill...." It went on to give a link to fake website with a plausible looking URL.

Similar frauds have included communications from what appears to be **TV licensing, HM Revenue and Customs (HMRC),** the **Gov.uk** website and the **DVLA.**

The HMRC scam might suggest that you are **owed a tax**

rebate, or that you owe **unpaid taxes** and are at risk of incurring penalty fines. Some even suggest you may be arrested. These scams often peak around the time people are submitting their tax returns and are expecting some communication from HMRC, but HMRC will never email, message or text you with information about tax due or owed or ask for personal information.

Another scam purported to come from the **National Crime Agency**, via a serious-sounding and alarming phone message suggesting that your **National Insurance number** had been compromised. The message asks you to agree to be connected to an 'agent', who is in fact a fraudster.

There are also scams from people pretending to be the police, saying that they need help in a **fraud investigation**. These can become very elaborate and draw people into an entirely fictional world of apparent intrigue, but the only aim is to extract money from you.

Scams where you are emotionally involved

Online dating has given rise to an epidemic of fraud in which people become involved with someone they believe to be a real person. They develop what appears to be a genuine **online relationship** and become **emotionally attached** to the person – sometimes deeply attached. At that point the fraudster cynically invents some reason why they need money: for the airfare to come to meet in person; because a relative has become seriously unwell and needs money for medical treatment, or for some other plausible-sounding reason.

There has been a rash of similar scams known generally as **'Hi mum'** scams, where a parent gets a message from what seems to be their son or daughter who urgently need money to get them out of some difficult and sometimes truly distressing-sounding situation, possibly in a foreign country. The scammer invents some reason why the message is not coming from the usual phone number. They may even have been able to learn the name of the son or daughter from social media; everything else is nonsense. It is easy to get caught up in such scams because our first reaction is one of real panic and the irresistible urge to solve the problem and make our children safe.

At a lower emotional temperature, you may also get emails that seem to come from someone who is in your social circle – perhaps appearing to be an **old college friend** – who is now being held captive by a drug cartel in South America (for example) and urgently needs some cash to pay their ransom. The email may well stress how they wouldn't normally reach out like this, but they don't know where else to turn. Again, scammers have probably been able to get details of your old college from social media and have used this to create a fake but plausible spoof email sender's address.

Microsoft, software etc.

There have been scams where people purporting to be calling from **Microsoft** or other **software providers** offer to help fix issues with your computer. They may ask you to give them **remote access** to your computer or to **visit a link** to a fake website. If they are given control of your screen, they may display normal system messages that they claim are proof of the existence of the so-called 'problem'. The fix to the fictitious problem will almost certainly involve your downloading some 'patch' which is in fact **malware** that may freeze your computer until a ransom is paid or, more damagingly, may allow them to steal personal and financial information directly from your computer.

You won't be surprised to know that companies like Microsoft – who are quite hard to contact if you have a genuine problem – do not proactively call people up asking if you have a problem! Don't be afraid to be 'rude' to someone who starts asking suspicious questions about your computer: end the call and hang up.

Lotteries and prizes

This is simple but effective. You are told you have **won** a large sum of money, but need to make some payment or give access to your bank account in order to claim the prize. Our excitement at our apparent windfall makes us less cautious than we should be.

Personal loans

Fraudsters may be able to obtain the contact details of people who have been looking for **a personal loan.** The victim is contacted with details of some attractive loan offer which requires payment of an initial fee – something which is plausible but would only happen in reality once a loan has been agreed with a lender and you have set up, for example, a direct debit for regular repayments. The advance payment is made, but the promised loan never turns up.

Amazon

This is a common scam. You might receive a recorded message on your phone or a call from a real person saying there is some **problem with your accoun**t that needs urgent attention. They may threaten to **close your account** unless you 'confirm' your payment details and other personal details.

There are also email and text scams that try to persuade you to click on links that lead to a fake version of what seems to be your Amazon account. They may attach what seems to be an invoice for something expensive that you haven't ordered and say that you need to help them resolve the 'problem'. The aim is to get you to enter details that will give them access to either your bank account or your Amazon account.

If you find yourself having this kind of conversation, end the call and go to your Amazon account. If there is a real problem, it will be displayed there.

Parcel delivery

We all have parcels delivered regularly—increasingly so since the pandemic. A text arrives to say that **you were out** when the delivery driver called or that there is some small **shipping fee** outstanding. Once you click through to the link, you are asked for your personal details – often a suspicious number of details including, for example, your date of birth. If you are being asked to pay money, the sums of money for the alleged 'fee' are small and you may be **tempted to pay**; it doesn't seem likely that someone would go to the trouble to cheat you out of a few pounds. This is part of the scam, which is not about taking a few pounds off you: the real aim is to collect enough personal information for identity theft or to be able to contact you again in future with a convincing level of detail to tempt you into other more damaging scams.

Banks

Bank scams can be very sophisticated and convincing. You are contacted by someone who says they are calling from **your**

bank – perhaps via apparently real phone numbers or texts. A text may offer you a link to a fake version of the bank's website which asks you to **enter your login details.** Which the fraudsters capture and can then use to access your bank account. A phone call may persuade you to give your PIN numbers or passwords. Very often the fraudsters will pose as bank **security experts** who say they are worried about unusual activity in your account such as new payees or a suspicious looking transfer. They may say that it is essential to set up some new 'safe' account because your old account has been compromised and persuade you to **transfer your money** to this new fraudulent account.

A number of banks have come together to create 'Stop Scams UK' and have created a new 159 hot line. If you find yourself having some kind of communication with anyone claiming to be your bank, they recommend that you end the conversation immediately and dial 159, which will connect you securely with your real bank to confirm whether there is or is not a real issue with your account.

Investment

There are various **investment scams** which appear to offer very **attractive rates** of return, perhaps in topical sectors such as green energy or crypto currency, probably in the form of some 'bond'.

They may claim to be from a firm you have never heard of or may pretend to be representing a well-known institution. If it is the latter, use that institution's website to check if the investment offer is mentioned there. The fraudsters will almost certainly ask you to make a 'push' payment from your bank account of the kind you use to transfer money to a family member or to pay small companies. Legitimate investment houses will not do this, they will always use direct debits or debit card payments. An excellent rule of thumb is, "If it sounds too good to be true, it probably is."

In general, if you are uneasy about any communication, don't get dragged into doing anything you are uncomfortable about. Nothing is actually 'urgent' – if there is a problem, a genuine organisation will always help resolve the issue over time.

If you receive any phone call you are uncomfortable with, hang up. Again, any genuine organisation will be very understanding. Just call back on the normal number and check to see if you need to do anything. Never use a number the caller has given you or let them 'put you through' to someone else.

Never click on links in texts or emails you are not entirely confident about. Look carefully at the email address of a suspicious email pretending to come from some person or organisation you know – you may see that the 'real' email address is not what it claims to be.

Anything that involves your bank account can be very dangerous; your bank will never contact you asking for a PIN or password or say they need to collect one of your bank cards. If you have any doubts, hang up and call your bank on the usual number or call the new 159 hotline.

Part III

Chapter 13: The Psychology of Money

As a financial adviser, my goal is to help people make use of their money to increase their day-to-day happiness and freedom. Rather than being controlled by their wealth it should liberate them. The more we can understand what makes us tick and why we sometimes behave in irrational ways, the **better financial decisions** we can make. We recognise that our psychological makeup and our emotions have a big effect on our personal lives and on our relationships; it is perhaps not so obvious that they can have an equally important impact on our financial decisions – but they can and do.

I've read a lot of books on and around this subject. In this chapter I've put together the major highlights I think everyone should know and have specifically referenced a few of my favourites which effectively set the bar for each topic.

You may have read a book called The Chimp Paradox by sports psychologist Steve Peters. I highly recommend it, if not, as it perfectly describes how we think, which in turn dictates our actions. Peters explains that the human brain can be thought of as being divided into three parts: the frontal, the limbic and the parietal. The limbic system is the more ancient part of the brain, and it is concerned with survival (food, fight or flight and reproduction). The frontal system is concerned with decision making and rational thought based on facts and evidence. The parietal system processes information from the senses and constructs our understanding of the world around us. Peters calls these 'the chimp' (limbic), 'the human' (frontal) and 'the computer' (parietal). He points out that these three parts of the brain are often in conflict with each other, pulling us towards making very different decisions, and he argues that it is very useful to think of our 'chimp' as a real chimpanzee that we have to try to control, recognising when it is driving us to behave in a way that is not rational and not in our best interest.

Our inner chimp is driven by emotions, and we respond to these much faster than we do to the rational decisions of our 'human' brain. The limbic brain is concerned with survival, so it reacts extremely quickly to anything it finds threatening – five times faster than our logical brain can respond. Everything we experience is in effect filtered through this system, which acts as a kind of gatekeeper, and the gatekeeper is not rational: it is angry, jealous, overconfident, fearful and greedy. By the time any impression gets through to our slower, rational brains, it has already been given an emotional content by our limbic system: our 'chimp'. It tells us that this new input is scary, or frightening, or should make us jealous, even when this may not be justified by reality.

In Peters' account, the chimp is quick to jump to an opinion, thinks in black and white, tends to see things in paranoid and catastrophic terms and is irrational and emotive. Which you may recognise as being a lot like you on a bad day! The 'human' brain, in contrast, is rational, evidence based, sees things in terms of context and perspective, and is capable of dealing with shades of grey and making balanced judgements.

As we saw earlier, if someone crashes into our car, our inner chimp responds immediately with fear and then anger. But if we find the driver of the other car is rushing someone to hospital or there are other extenuating circumstances, we can quickly calm down. Our logical, human brain is taking over from the chimp. The same is true, only in a far more subtle way, of many everyday reactions. We make some straightforward comment to our partner or a colleague at work, and they respond in a way that we interpret as a criticism. Perhaps we feel they are being sarcastic. Our inner chimp is immediately alarmed at this 'threat' and lashes out with some hostile response. Things quickly escalate into a row or perhaps leave both parties simmering with suppressed indignation.

Sound familiar? The rational response, of course, would be to decide that nothing was meant by the response or, if we thought it was an issue that should be discussed, to talk about it calmly to see if there was a genuine issue. It is possible to train ourselves to be more logical and less driven by our inner chimp, but there are also times when 'our emotions get the better of us' and we struggle to stay calm and reasonable.

Emotional ups and downs are common in financial markets, and to understand this and the have ability to think logically at these times is an incredibly useful tool for investors during times of both market highs and lows. The parietal system – our' 'computer brain' – can be harnessed to help us act on autopilot based on **learned behaviour**. As we go through life, we learn how to deal logically with certain situations because of our previous experiences. We learn that grass is generally green, and if it is brown or yellow on occasions, we realise that there must be a drought. We don't worry (though our inner chimp might) that grass has suddenly turned yellow forever and the world will never be the same again. In the same way, we can train our computer brain to take over in various financial decisions and think, 'We've seen this situation before, and this was the best option to take.' Financial crashes would be a perfect example. It is easy to become fearful when markets go down, but experience tells us that markets always recover, often remarkably quickly. Our brown and yellow lawns turn green again when it rains. Our relationship with **money is very personal**, which means we often make **emotional rather than rational decisions** about money matters, but it is the logical choices, not emotional ones, that will deliver the financial results we want.

The fear of starting new things, such as different types of investment, tends to hold people back. Fear versus optimism can be quite troublesome because **going into the unknown** is always difficult. The more I work with people on cashflow modelling and so on, the **better informed** they become about their finances and the decisions they need to make. They then have more **control and influence over their mindset** and the direction in which their life is going. This is because it helps us see the bigger picture, which provides perspective. Then we can run different models which look at the most likely outcomes but also the worst-case scenarios so that clients know what to do if things don't necessarily go to plan.

As people approach **retirement**, they are often worried about spending their money because they are afraid it will run out. People often acknowledge that they are not thinking rationally, but it can be very hard to control our inner chimp in this instance, because it has gone into 'catastrophic' mode and is telling us we have to make sure there is enough food in the larder. I find it helps people to work through how much money they have and how much they actually need. Most of the time, they will find they have more than enough. Our investments may also become more important to us when we have retired, especially if we are drawing an income from them, and we may find ourselves feeling more anxious about swings in the market. When we begin to understand the psychology behind what is influencing our decisions, that can be a powerful help.

Biases

There are a number of common **biases** we all exhibit that psychologists have identified. Some of these are emotional and have to do with our inner chimp versus our rational mind. Others are caused more by the fact that most of us are bad at working out the real odds in many common situations: our emotions lead us to 'feel' that something is our best course of action, when in fact the odds are stacked the other way.

Loss aversion is a good example. Research shows that the pain of losing money is twice as powerful as the pleasure of gaining it in the first place. In one experiment, people were given a notional £100. They were then asked to choose between a certain loss of £50 (meaning they got to keep £50), or the flip of a coin to determine whether they kept or lost the whole £100. Most people favoured the flip of the coin because there was a 50% chance they might lose nothing (avoiding a definite loss), even though there was the same chance of their losing everything. Faced with the reverse of this – winning £50 with certainty or flipping a coin with the chance to win nothing or £100 – most people take the first option: a certain gain of £50. People are more loss averse than they are risk averse; they would prefer to gamble than accept a loss, but they will decline to gamble if offered a definite gain.

In the same way, people only tend to talk about their successes and not their losses. They are vocal when stocks they have invested in do well, but not so loud when there is a drop off. Even when markets are doing well, financial advisors will always recommend that people diversify their investment into some safer options, in case the market turns downwards, but people are often reluctant: why take money out of something that is performing well? When markets are doing badly, on the other hand, people are very keen to get rid of their 'bad' investments to avoid further losses, even though there is a very good chance that those investments are currently undervalued and will rally.

This might be a good place to recap on some of the more common 'biases' that psychologists have identified. I suspect you will recognise many of them!

> **Hindsight bias.** Once something has happened, we tend to believe it was obvious all along. *"I should have seen this coming!"*

> **Herding.** The tendency of people to follow the crowd and make similar investments instead of doing their own research. *"I got a great stock tip from a friend of a friend!"*

Overconfidence/overestimation. When someone's confidence in their own ability exceeds their actual performance, this can lead to excessive risk-taking. *"This can't miss!"*

Authority bias. The tendency to trust the opinions of authority figures in the belief they are likely to be correct. *"They must know what they're talking about!"*

Hyperbolic discounting. The preference for immediate gratification or a short-term reward, and the tendency to underestimate costs in the future. *"I can always start saving later."*

Myopic loss aversion. Selling off good investments as a result of short-term losses, even when they are sound long-term investments. *"I check my account every hour!"*

New era thinking. The idea that a current boom is an exception because it is new and exciting, even when exactly similar booms have gone bust in the past. *"This time is different!"*

Affect heuristic. Making emotionally driven decisions, also known as 'gut feeling', when choosing investments. *"It just feels right!"*

Status quo bias. A tendency to prefer the current state of affairs when faced with various possible alternatives. *"Rebalance my portfolio – what for?"*

Hot hand fallacy. The belief that previous successes - for example, in gambling or in sports or stock picking - increase the likelihood of subsequent successes. *"I'm on a winning streak right now!"*

There are several other relevant biases to be aware of. **Confirmation bias** is the tendency to take note of information that validates our decisions and ignore information that contradicts them. This can be a very powerful effect; even when there is growing evidence that we have made a mistake, we seize on anything that suggests we were right, and it takes prominence in our minds.

Anchoring is another. If we are uncertain of the value of something and someone puts forward a suggestion, we are likely to estimate that the actual value is relatively close to the original suggestion, even when it is completely wide of the mark. In the same way, we tend to cling to points of reference, such as the original purchase price of something, even when that has become irrelevant.

Mental accounting is something I come across on a daily basis. People mentally sort their money into different 'accounts' and are reluctant to spend money from one 'account' or another, even when this is obviously in their best interest. People will pay high interest on a credit card debt for several months, for example, because they are reluctant to move money out of a savings account, even when there is no penalty for doing so and no need to borrow the money. Essentially this is an act of borrowing money at a high rate to put into savings at a lower rate. Nobody would rationally do this but if the money is already saved, it can be easy to fall into this trap. In a similar way, people are sometimes happy to spend money they see as a 'windfall' but reluctant to spend money that came from an inheritance.

Media sensationalism

The media influences people by using sensationalism to constantly talk about disasters and other terrible things. I tend to refer to it as the **EastEnders effect.** Everyone knows that in soap operas there is always something dramatic or disastrous happening. This creates an element of fear in the viewers' minds, compounded by the cliff-hanger at the end of every episode. Viewers need to know what happens next, so they keep coming back. If the story was like real life where most people are happy most of the time, no one would watch the next episode because there would be no drama. The media are cleverly designed to feed those centres of fear and panic because they crave our attention, which is the media's financial lifeblood.

The media are also good at grabbing our attention by using inflammatory or **hyperbolic language.** A sensational headline captures our attention, but when we read more, we realise that nothing very earth shattering has actually happened. Sometimes almost literally nothing has happened, but the writer has managed to create some attention-grabbing story out of thin air.

There is a constant tendency to stir up **controversy** because it engages people. **Social media** are dangerously good at this, feeding people news stories and comments that they know will make them angry via algorithms to encourage them to respond, leading to **rumour cascades** in which everyone is getting more and more upset and angry about relatively insignificant things. Social media are also very good at creating **narrative fallacies,** where the fact that certain events have happened is imbued with a false sense of cause and effect. **Conspiracy theories** are the perfect example.

Some media channels provide **infotainment** where factual reporting is secondary to entertainment value. Another thing to be aware of, especially on social media, is **context stripping,** where an image or report may be shared without any clear context or information about its origin. There is also an oversimplification of **good versus evil**, where any nuance is stripped out and one group of people is portrayed as 'the good guys' and the others as 'the bad guys'. This is happening more and more in political debate, where people with different political beliefs are depicted as being monsters, rather than as people with different political views.

All of this media 'noise' plays to our inner chimp, making us more fearful than we should be of things that are not especially dangerous, or can sweep us up in some craze that has little foundation in reality. Every boom and bust is driven by a contagion of popular feeling, and modern media are especially good at spreading these contagions. When we make important financial decisions, it is hugely important to avoid reacting to scare stories and to try to filter out the important bits of information from the noise. Financial advisors can be extremely helpful here, as this is what they are trained to do.

There are a lot of **unregulated people offering financial advice** who put videos on Facebook, TikTok or Instagram. Some of it might be useful, but mostly it is clickbait designed to pull you in and sell you something. The product they are pushing may not necessarily be a financial product and could be something entirely unrelated – but the financial angle has been used to catch your attention. I would like to see a greater level of regulation in this field, because of the potentially serious consequences of financial misinformation.

Emotional responses

The **seduction of pessimism** is another interesting aspect of the psychology of money: the idea that people who are more pessimistic about the world will eventually be proved right. Pessimists are literally waiting for something bad to happen, often fuelled by media predictions of doom and gloom. But remember that the reality of the financial world is that markets go up 75% of the time, and down only 25% of the time; over the long term they are unbeaten. Being aware of the emotional triggers that can catch us out is important because they can throw us into overspending modes or investment panics without any real foundation.

It is important that people should be able to **self-invest**, and many people get a great deal of satisfaction from this and will save themselves some money in management fees. But the **larger the amount of money**, the more **emotive** people will often be in terms of managing it. Top fund managers are able to deal with transactions worth billions of pounds and keep a cool head. Most people are OK with a sum of perhaps £10,000 or £20,000, but when it approaches perhaps £50,000 or £100,000, they understandably start to get a bit jumpy. This is especially true if the money represents their entire pension, or they have built up an ISA over 20 years and everything relies on it; their concerns become exaggerated; the size of the pot of money involved increases the risk of bad decisions being made and is a very good reason to consider getting professional advice.

Sentimentality can impact finances too. In the last decade, more and more people have inherited a stock portfolio. There was a move to encourage wider share ownership back in the 1980s and 90s when various public utilities such as gas and electricity were privatised, and many of us will inherit a share portfolio from our parents. People tend to behave differently with these portfolios because they are aware they have been built up over time and they don't want to take a risk with them. They tend to leave them just as they were when they were inherited. It is a little bit like holding onto our parents, or as if they are stockholding from the grave. People think very differently about money they win in the lottery or a bonus they get from work.

Many people will also hold **different values** to their parents, especially regarding the environment and ESG (Environmental, Social and Governance) investments. They feel uncomfortable about inheriting shares in companies like Shell or BP and struggle to come to terms with it, even though they may be very sound investments. But if holding those shares is making them feel uncomfortable, I encourage people to make their own choice. I am sure that their parents wouldn't have intended to insist that those shares were kept forever. The thing to remember is that people want their children to benefit from the proceeds so it can be spent by them on enjoying their lives, making it easier and more enjoyable.

I have come across numerous clients who have inherited money that is intended to be passed on to the grandchildren. The intention is for it to be used for their grandchildren's house purchases, but the grandchildren might be only 3 years old, and will not be able to buy a house until they are at least 18 – and even then, are unlikely to know where they want to put down roots and live longer term. As we saw earlier, the average first-time buyer is now 33 years old. But many people hold on to the cash because they are fearful about doing the wrong thing or choosing the wrong investment but then hold this money as **cash** for a decade or more and the value is seriously eroded by inflation resulting in a guaranteed loss in purchasing power.

Envy can have a big impact on someone's life situation and can even lead to financial ruin. There are always other people who appear to be more successful than us, with bigger houses and a lifestyle to match. People who are envious of others tend to want to chase that dream or status can end up taking risks they cannot afford in an effort to catch up, rather than considering what would be best for them personally.

It is always worth reflecting on the things we do to understand the reasons behind our decisions. Are we buying a bigger house or sending our children to a private school just because other people are doing it? It is not healthy, emotionally or financially, to compare our lives to those of other people, even our family, friends or colleagues. It's as simple as that.

Risk

An excellent book by Thomas Erikson called Surrounded by Idiots categorises people into four different **personality types**: red, green, blue and yellow. Blue people are very analytical and tend to be more introverted and risk-averse; red people are often entrepreneurs who throw caution to the wind and take risks. Yellow people are very sociable and optimistic and tend to be driven by instincts and gut feeling. Green people are very balanced and conciliatory and avoid conflict. These traits are inherent to us. Understand our personality type helps us understand our attitude to risk and the barriers we face in our decision making. I'd recommend this book to anyone, if they have time, in order to improve their understanding of themselves, their thought processes and that of colleagues, friends and family.

Habits

Some of the things that we do are a result of habits. The book *Atomic Habits* by James Clear is about **building good habits** and breaking bad ones. The idea is that there are four stages of habit formation: **unconscious incompetence** (being unaware of a habit); **conscious incompetence** (aware of the habit but finding it difficult to change); **conscious competence** (changing the habit with conscious effort); **unconscious competence** (the new habit becomes automatic).

The brain goes through these different phases, especially when it is adapting to major life events such as becoming a parent or retiring. Suddenly there is a new normal when the old habits are no longer relevant, and the brain sets out on a new learning path to build new habits. At first, it is difficult for us to adapt as the brain expects us to keep doing what we've been doing. It takes a lot of practice to form a new habit (between 13 and 20 repetitions). But once people practice what is called **habit stacking**, this helps to bypass the emotive brain. The more effortless something becomes, the less people think about it and the new habit becomes automatic. The same is true of getting rid of bad habits. This idea links back to The Chimp Paradox and Steve Peters' description of the 'computer brain' that allows us to automate certain habits of thought. It typically takes people around 18 months to forget old, automated habits and settle into the era of change.

It is very useful to become aware of any financial tendencies we may have ('conscious incompetence') and to put in the effort needed to change. With enough effort and practice, we can move to conscious competence and then to the ideal state of unconscious competence, where we automatically take the most advantageous course of action.

The art of spending

When we think about 'bad' financial habits, we tend to think of the obvious things: failing to save enough money or selling off fundamentally sound investments in a panic when there is a market downturn, for example. But, perverse as it may sound, people can also have problems spending money they can afford and 'should' be spending, or find themselves spending money for 'bad' reasons, or in ways that don't give them as much pleasure as it should.

Morgan Housel, the author of The Psychology of Money, wrote an excellent blog, "The Art and Science of Spending Money."[17] He tells the story of the famous American CEO, Jack Welch, who made a fortune from his ultra-successful leadership of the multinational conglomerate GE. Welch had a heart attack in later life and was rushed to hospital, but survived. In a subsequent interview, Welch was asked what he was thinking as he was receiving treatment and wondering if these were his

[17] The Art and Science of Spending Money · Collab Fund

last moments on earth. His main thought, Welch told his interviewer, was, "Damn it, **I didn't spend enough money**." Welch explained that he had had quite a poor childhood, and it had made him **habitually frugal**. He promised himself that from then on, he would 'never buy a bottle of wine for less than a hundred dollars.'

In his blog, Housel lists a number of 'bad' spending habits and encourages us to adopt good spending habits instead. He writes about Jack Welch's problem – an upbringing that led him to be careful with money, even when he had more money that he could spend in a lifetime, or several lifetimes. Housel calls this **frugality inertia** – the inability to stop the frugal habits of an earlier phase in our lives. He also talks about **revenge spending**, by which he means people spending money ostentatiously because they grew up poor and want to show off their new wealth, and about being **entrapped by spending** – how people with a lot of money can come to 'devote themselves to **expense regardless of pleasure**'. Housel tells the story of George Vanderbilt, a member of the incredibly wealthy Vanderbilt family that had built fortune from steamboat and railroad businesses in the nineteenth century as America began to modernise. George Vanderbilt built a huge 40-bedroom mansion in North Carolina but hardly ever spent time there because it was so inconvenient as a place to actually live in. The upkeep of the house and its 400 staff nearly bankrupted him.

Housel points out that we tend to get more **pleasure** from spending our money when it has been an **effort** to acquire it, and people can find they get less and less pleasure from spending their money in the obvious ways. The answer usually lies in re-examining the things that are **truly important** to us and what we see as our purpose in life. Many wealthy people find fulfilment in devoting their money and energy to projects that genuinely matter to them and bring them real satisfaction. Passing money on to future generations or to charitable causes is another satisfying use of money, but no one will begrudge you getting as much pleasure as you can out of money well-spent in your lifetime.

There are many ways to **experiment with spending** to discover what brings you the most pleasure. If, for example, you find that something quite expensive is what you genuinely most enjoy – like staying at a top-class hotel, for example – then you might find that you can cut out on a lot of the spending that doesn't actually bring you much pleasure, and focus your spending instead on the things that genuinely make you happy, even if they are relatively expensive. This applies to all kinds of expenditure: you might find that buying works of art, drinking fine wine or learning to fly a plane are the things that make you truly happy. Now you can stop spending money on a lot of other things and focus on the things you know bring you most satisfaction!

One final idea from Housel: he tells an apocryphal story about a committee charged with approving three spending applications: £10 million for new nuclear power station; £400 for a new bike shed or £20 on refreshments for people. The committee spends the most time debating the £20 spent on refreshments. £10 million is too much money to think about and the whole thing is too complex for debate; most people had some kind of opinion about what the ideal bike shed should look like and are keen to contribute; everyone had an opinion about what kind of food and drink should be served as refreshments and a lively debate ensues. The moral of the story is that we tend to devote far too much time worrying about **minor financial decisions**, and not enough time looking at the **big picture** as to whether our financial situation is set up for long-term success. We worry about the £20 decision when it is the equivalent of the £10 million decision that really matters.

When making financial decisions my challenge to you is to take a step back, consider the bigger picture and reflect more on the why as well as the end result you are trying to achieve with any investment. Think about why you are investing: will the action get you closer to achieving your aim ? If you have already invested, think about why you're holding the investment and, when you come to sell it, why you are selling it.

Shortcuts

- Understand yourself, your lifestyle and have conviction in your own goals to make the best decisions.
- **Logical** choices, not emotional ones, will deliver the **financial results** we want.
- We can make better financial decision when we understand the **psychology** behind what holds us back or drives us to do things and spot our emotive triggers.
- People are more **loss-averse** than they are risk averse; consider if this is holding you back.
- Psychologists have identified many **biases** that lead us to make instinctive decisions that are not logically or statistically justified. Take time to consider your actions before making them.
- All media coverage tends towards **sensationalism** and hyperbole, making the world seem more dangerous and extreme than it is; is this news truly significant to you or helping you to make a rational decision?
- **Social media** tends to feed people stories that make them **angry or upset**, because this engages them; this leads to political antagonism, rumour cascades, narrative fallacies and conspiracy theories. It's the modern version of hearsay and tips in the pub, this is not where the best investment ideas are conceived.

- We are all prone to negative key **emotional responses** in financial matters, including pessimism, sentimentality, envy and greed. Minimising this and using your logic pays dividends.

- It is important to understand how our **personality type** affects our attitude to **risk taking** and other financial decisions; after any event, consider how this affected you and, if it happened again, whether you would think, feel or act the same way. This will naturally evolve over time with more experience and education.

- With practice we can create good, automated **habits based on our learned experience**; these help to change and improve our previously emotionally driven responses.

- Money is there to be **spent**, passed on to other people or to support good causes; get as much genuine **pleasure** as possible from your money.

Market movements reflect human decision-making, with all its attendant intellectual limitations and emotional biases.

However, when markets are moving quickly – either upwards or down – it is all too tempting to make rash decisions driven by emotion rather than logic. And those decisions may pose a serious threat to your long-term financial health. During times of rising market volatility, investors should be reminded of the benefits of looking beyond such short-term market fluctuations and avoid the temptation to try to time the market.

Retaining a long-term perspective is the best protection against impulsive or irrational decision-making.

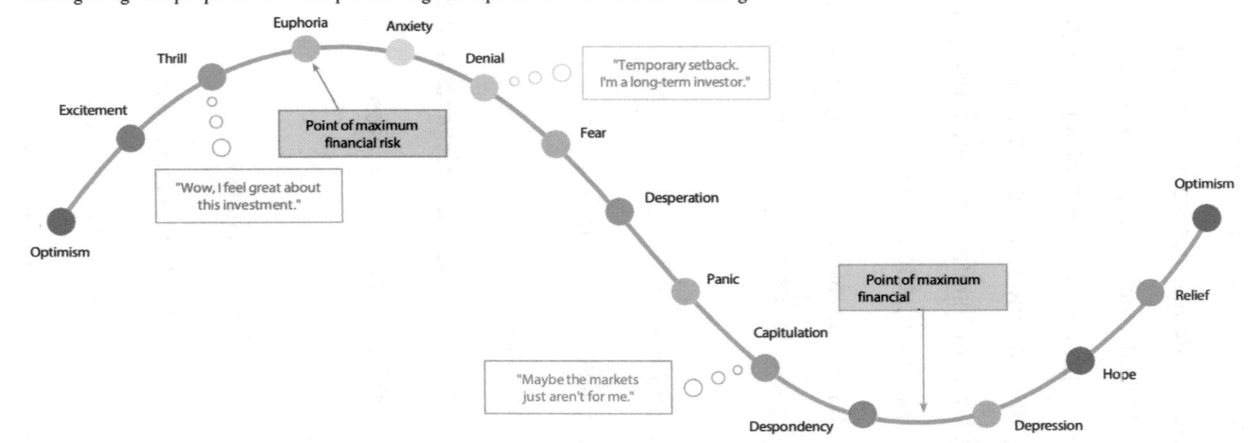

Investors tend to struggle to stay level-headed when the markets take a dip. Investing based on emotion (greed or fear) is the main reason why so many people are buying at market tops and selling at market bottoms.

Chapter 14: Goals and Goal Planning

As a financial advisor I am in the business of wealth management. People create wealth, and we help them to make best use of that wealth and use it to achieve their goals. We've talked throughout this book about the different things we are all likely to want and need at different stages of our lives. In this chapter, I would like to focus on **setting goals** and how we can go about **achieving** those goals.

To offer some food for thought about setting your own personal goals, these are the 10 most common goals people tell me about.

1. *Travel more*
2. *Achieve financial independence*
3. *Own a holiday home*
4. *Spend more time with friends and relatives*
5. *Work less or start a new career*
6. *Retire early*
7. *Start their own business*
8. *Become debt and mortgage free*
9. *Give more money to good causes*
10. *Move to a different country*

Those are all entirely sensible goals and achieving even a few of them would make most of us happy. Interestingly, the most obvious goals are the ones most easily thought of, but they are not necessarily the **only goals** in our lives, or even the **most important goals.** Most people would say an important goal in their lives is to be able to give their children a good start in life, support them financially at various times throughout their lives and leave them a good inheritance. But that is so 'obvious', that most people don't list it as a goal when they are asked what they want to achieve.

Another 'obvious' goal is being able to sustain and hopefully improve our current lifestyle. The importance of this goal is often understated; if we know for certain we can continue to maintain an enjoyable lifestyle for the rest of our lives, a lot of other things might become a kind of 'icing on the cake'. We might like to travel more and own a holiday home, but if we are able to continue our current lifestyle with a holiday or two a year and the ability to go and stay in a hotel or a rented villa when we feel like it, that might well be enough.

Other goals are related to our self-development and might be hard to express. The goals of 'starting a new career' or 'starting my own business' may hint at this. What people might mean when they state those as goals is that they've always dreamed of being a musician or an artist, or of running their own business teaching people to windsurf. Sometimes we think these are just wild fancies: pipedreams. But maybe we should take goals like this more seriously – some people achieve their dreams, after all.

The most 'obvious' goal of all might be to stay fit and healthy and to experience happiness and satisfaction in our lives. That's probably the most important goal of all, and there are real and concrete things we can do to give ourselves the best chance of achieving them. Many philosophers have argued that **happiness** is everyone's **ultimate goal**, and that everything else is just a means to the real end of achieving happiness.

Here are some useful tips about goal setting:

- *Decide on the* ***priority*** *of each goal: which are the most important to you?*
- *Put a* ***timeframe*** *on it: when do you want to achieve it?*
- *Put a* ***cost*** *on it: how much capital or income do you need to make it happen?*
- *Plot a financial* ***route*** *to your destination: how much money do you need to put aside each month to achieve your goal?*
- *Decide how much* ***risk*** *you are prepared to take: do you*

want to work slowly and steadily towards the goal or are you prepared to risk a great deal to achieve it sooner?

Achieving **financial independence** is a fundamental goal. We all need to achieve this by the time we can retire. We want to be confident that we can support ourselves and have an enjoyable lifestyle when we are no longer earning money. The question really becomes: how soon do you want to stop working? I'll talk more about financial independence in a moment.

To achieve our goals, we need a **financial plan**; we need to **invest**, because no matter how much money we have, we still need to invest something now to achieve a future goal; and we need to **manage our behaviour**. We're only human, after all, and we represent the biggest risk to our own future success! We might understand that we need to do something, but whether or not we actually do it is another thing altogether.

Financial planning can help reduce the inevitable risks we face. **Insurance** will protect you and your family if you suffer an illness or your life is cut short; **investing** money will protect you if your life is long and healthy. It is possible, at different stages of our lives, to have **too much money, too little money,** or **just the right amount.** It is important to **review** our finances constantly to see where we are at any point in time.

We mentioned financial independence earlier. An acronym many people use is **FIRE: Financial Independence Retire Early.**

I'd like to offer a useful rule of thumb to work out how much capital you need to build up to be able to retire early: work out how much you need each month to sustain the lifestyle you want and multiply it by 300. So, for example, if you need £1,000 per month to live comfortably, you need £300,000 in capital to become financially independent. It's easier to work from what you need monthly as this is how we historically get paid and is a spending and budgeting habit that is hard to move away from.

The logic behind this is quite simple: it is generally accepted that you should be able to manage your investments so that you can draw down 4% p.a. while still allowing your capital to grow enough to keep pace with inflation. £1,000 per month is £12,000 p.a. Multiply this annual amount by 25 to represent the necessary 4% drawdown (100/4 = 25). So multiplying your required monthly sum of £1,000 by 300 (12 x 25) gives a sum of £300,000. That gives you the amount of capital you need to live on typically for the rest of your life without running down your capital and allowing the income drawn to keep pace with inflation.

To become financially independent relatively early in life will require **sacrifices**. Ideally, you should be putting aside an amount of money each month that is slightly **uncomfortable**; it should be a stretch. We talked earlier about the importance of automating your saving habits. For example, as we suggested earlier, every time you get a pay rise, **increase your pension contributions by 1%** of your salary and save as much of the rest as you can manage. You may well find that you can live comfortably without the extra money because you hardly notice it's 'gone' – and your pension and savings will grow steadily and healthily.

The options are really quite simple: you can spend less and invest more. It's not everyone's favourite, but it works! Or you can earn more and invest more from the new additional income. Or, of course, you can earn more, spend less and invest even more.

I've said this several times in this book because it is very important: even when you are investing as much as possible to build up enough capital to make you financially independent, it is essential to still maintain an **emergency fund** of accessible savings. Otherwise, if some small crisis occurs, you will need to withdraw investment funds to deal with it and, as we saw earlier, investments work best over relatively long cycles that avoid the inevitable peaks and troughs of the investment market. You don't want to be forced to withdraw investment funds at a bad time just because there has been an unexpected crisis.

Once you have built up enough capital to be able to retire, that is a good moment to decide whether you are still living in the right property for your new phase of life. Perhaps you could **downsize.** Or, if you want to keep the property and leave it as part of your inheritance, you could consider **equity release**, where a lender takes a mortgage on the property, releases some of the value of your property in cash, charges you interest, and is repaid the capital when the property is finally sold. That means you are leaving less of your property's value to the next generation, but the capital released may allow you to maintain the lifestyle you want, which your children will not begrudge you. If you take capital out of your property via an equity release loan but do not or cannot afford to make the regular interest payments on the loan, then compound interest begins to work against you: you start to pay interest on the interest owed for every year that the loan is outstanding, and debts can mount significantly. But equity release where you can afford the regular interest payments can be a useful way of freeing up capital. The amount of capital that must be repaid when the property is finally sold remains constant and does not mount up.

I find that clients are often resistant to the idea of leaving their current, probably unnecessarily large, property. But if I say to them, "If you move house, I will pay off your remaining mortgage and give you £100,000 in cash," they often see the issue in a different light. As we saw earlier, people get emotionally attached to properties as they are full of memories. But memories stay in the mind not in objects so you can take them with you. Many people also keep spare bedrooms so that they can put up occasional visitors 4-5 times per year, when it would be far cheaper and more sensible to pay for friends and family to stay in a nearby hotel after they have downsized to a property that suits their everyday needs far better and they can live happily for the other 360 days per year.

Finding the **motivation** needed to achieve the ideal result is critical. Very often we can recognise that something would be a sensible course of action, but that isn't enough to drive us to act. Setting goals helps us to better understand what is important to us, and take the actions needed to make things happen. Imagine yourself at some time in the near future and imagine also that **time and money are no obstacle.** Now ask yourself some key questions. What is the **first thing** you would do? What would you like to **add** to your life? What would you like to **get rid of** in your life? What hobbies do you really care about and would like to do more of? How do you define success in your working life? How would you define success in your **family life**? What would be the **ideal balance** in your life? One final useful and important question is to ask yourself is how you hope to be **remembered.** This may guide your actions in later life.

Once we have clarified our goals and gone through the process we talked about at the start of this chapter, prioritising our goals and putting a timeframe and a cost on them, then we can reverse engineer the process in financial terms to work out what we have to do to achieve those goals. We can use our **financial GPS** to plot the route to the future we want.

The wealth of time

Wealth is an interesting concept. Being '**wealthy**' tends to mean having a lot of money tied up in property or various other assets. Being '**rich**', on the other hand, tends to mean having a lot of cash flow so you can spend a lot of money all of the time. Wealthy people might have land and property and many assets, but live quite simple lives. Rich people can buy yachts and Lamborghinis, go to expensive restaurants, and buy designer label clothes. A lot of people would probably say that they wanted to be rich and to be able to spend money freely. But what they tend to do – wisely in my opinion – is to try to build wealth. It is an interesting exercise to ask yourself what you most want at different stages of your life. An older person might be less interested in cash flow and spending and be more concerned with accumulating and passing on their wealth. Younger people are likely to be more interested in having lots of cash to spend. The good news is that it is nearly always possible to **turn wealth into income**: renting out property, for example, or moving investments into income-producing assets that will deliver the necessary annual return. It's like having a full water tower; when you get thirsty, you can simply turn on the tap.

One thing we tend to talk less about, but which is incredibly important if we are to lead happy and fulfilled lives, is the **wealth of time**. We have talked about the increasing likelihood of people living to be 100 years old. That is 1200 months, 5200 weeks, 36,400 days, or 873,600 hours. That's a lot of hours, but it's still a finite number. Time is precious; the clock is ticking. If you can achieve some of your goals sooner rather than later, what is that worth? Who can put a price on, perhaps, spending five more years doing what you really want to do as opposed to something that you are doing mainly to help you achieve your significant goals?

There are two simple lessons to take from this. The first, as we saw at the beginning of the chapter, is to think about the **timeframe** we set for achieving your goals and what sacrifices it is worth to accelerate that timeframe. The second is to **automate** as many as possible of our routine behaviours for managing our finances and building wealth.

I have met any number of people who over a lifetime have accumulated several bank accounts and ISAs, various savings accounts with different investment portfolios, several pension funds... and they struggle to manage them. It is incredibly time consuming. My strong recommendation is to **consolidate** everything you can. Have one or two bank accounts at a maximum; perhaps a personal account and a joint account with your partner. Have one instant access savings account and maybe two others that are fixed for a few years, because you still want a rolling amount of cash. Choose the one financial advisor who suits you best – you don't need two or three financial advisors. Some people like to see different, competing investment strategies, but a good advisor can invest your money with funds that have different investment strategies, spreading your opportunities and your risks. Otherwise, you are spending valuable time having essentially the same meetings with multiple advisors, only to achieve the same result. The best advisor is the one you want to see regularly as they challenge you but also listen to what you want to achieve. I would say however, that if you invest in a wide range of collectable items such as wine, art and cars, then it is better to seek out specialists in each area.

As I mentioned earlier, I highly recommend the book Essentialism by Greg McKeown, who describes his philosophy as 'the disciplined pursuit of less.' Find what you dislike or don't feel strongly about and cut that out of your life: say, 'No' to those things, but say, 'Hell, yes!', as McKeown puts it, to the things you truly enjoy. This allows you to put more of your time, energy and money into doing the things you love, because they are what bring you real pleasure and satisfaction.

We try to get the best possible 'returns' on our investments: **freedom and time** are probably the **highest possible returns** we can hope to get. Many people as they near the end of their lives realise that 'the little things' in their life – time spent with a partner, with family, with friends; time spent laughing – were actually 'the big things'. In the end, money simply gets converted into time: time spent with people we love; time spent on holiday; time spent in a house we love; time spent with beautiful objects we bought; time spent travelling and seeing the world. It really isn't about money; it's about time. You can die wealthy and pass your money on to the next generation – which is a satisfying thing to do. Or you could buy them things and gift them money in your lifetime and share in experiencing the pleasure it brings them. There's an amusing saying: 'Fly first class – or your kids will.' Money is meant to be spent, and will eventually get spent anyway, by someone. Indulge yourself a little while you have the chance.

Once you achieve financial independence and as you grow older, time will become more and more important, and new goals may become your priority. Perhaps you own houses that you rent out, and this has been a useful part of your financial planning – but perhaps now you would rather not have to spend the time that goes with dealing with tenants, finding new tenants when the previous tenants move out and dealing with maintenance issues and emergencies. Perhaps it is time to sell the properties and invest the proceeds or spend the money in some other way, freeing up your time and energy to spend more time with the family, for example. Perhaps you'd finally like to make that move to somewhere warmer and sunnier...

Your **financial advisor** can be very useful in helping you make these decisions, offering you an objective, non-judgmental opinion and playing devil's advocate, posing the sometimes difficult, 'What if...?' questions. They will also help you put the numbers on the goals you set yourself, telling you how much you need to put aside and how to actually achieve your goal: providing the financial GPS to guide you to your destination.

I find that people fall into one of four categories. There are people who don't know how to achieve their financial goals and simply need advice and guidance on what to do. Then there are people who do know what they can potentially do, but don't have the time to do it; they struggle even to find time for a meeting with their advisor to brief them on their situation. Then there are people who know what they can do and have the time to do it – but they hate doing their finances. They would rather be doing anything else. And finally, there are people who understand the value of financial advice – these are the people who may choose to have more than one advisor because they feel they are getting different perspectives and tapping into different financial strategies – but they also feel they should be making many of the key decisions about their investments themselves. They follow the markets closely and self-manage their funds, switching in and out of funds and individual stocks when they feel they have an insight into what is going up and what is coming down. They may also feel they are saving money by doing it themselves, which may be true if things go well, but can be very expensive if things go wrong. It's exciting, but it's also exhausting, and it can become a full-time job. That's why there are professional fund managers. My advice tends to be, ask yourself whether you would rather go through the rollercoaster experience of market peaks and troughs, living them moment by moment and ending up feeling a little dizzy and sick, or have professional fund managers manage your investments so you can sit back and enjoy the ride, travelling on the Orient Express instead of the rollercoaster.

I'll tell you an industry secret: financial advisors turn to their own colleagues for advice quite often as valuable sounding boards because we realise we don't always practise what we preach. We get emotionally invested in our own things, like everyone else. We don't always ask ourselves the hard questions. We don't always hold ourselves accountable so that we actually carry through with the things we know we should be doing. An expert, outside opinion from a colleague helps us see things clearly, answer the hard questions and see things through.

An advisor will spend time helping you achieve the goals you have set yourself while making your life as easy as possible so you can **enjoy the lifestyle** you want, not have to worry about things and then **leave the legacy** you want. They will remind you that '**tomorrow does come**' – that perhaps the day you have been waiting for all these years has finally arrived, and it is time to start spending your money.

Einstein once said that the cleverest people are not those who know everything, but those who know where to look for the answer or who to turn to for help. We employ experts to do our plumbing and fix our wiring and service our cars. Not everyone wants to spend time following the markets and reading the financial pages. Outsourcing the management of your finances to an advisor frees up your time so you can get on with doing what brings you most joy. Remember the Pareto principle: 20% of what you do in life brings you 80% of the joy you experience. The better you are able to identify the 20% that brings you joy and the more you can avoid the 80% that does not, the happier you will be.

I leave you with a final interesting thought: people with financial advisors retire on average five years earlier than people who don't. And I never had a client who had built up a large pension fund and a good investment portfolio and who was achieving their core goals in life who was unhappy about that.

Shortcuts

- Understanding our key **life goals** helps us **plan** to achieve them. Many will be realised early and others will then replace them and will also likely change over time. Its sensible to refresh your plans annually & reprioritise as needed.

- **Prioritise** your goals, put a **timeframe** and a **cost** on them, plan a **financial route** to achieve them and decide how much **risk** you are prepared to take to achieve them sooner.

- We all need to achieve **financial independence** to be able to retire: the question becomes: **how soon** do you want to retire?

- A good rule of thumb for the capital you need to allow you to be financially independent is to multiply the **monthly income you need** to live the lifestyle you want by **300** – for example, **£1,000 per month** requires a capital fund of **£300,000.** This would allow you to draw down income to support your lifestyle while your capital continues to keep pace with inflation.

- Achieving **early financial independence** will require an **uncomfortable** level of saving to invest; but it can be done!

- **Automate** your behaviours: put additional money into

savings accounts and your pension fund **every time you get a pay rise**. People often find it easier to do this as we're very good at adapting and working with budgets but rarely impose them on ourselves.

- Always keep an **emergency fund** so you don't need to access long-term investments to cope with a crisis.

- As you get older, consider **downsizing** your property or **releasing equity** to free up **capital**.

- When we are clear on our goals in life, we can use our **financial GPS** to plot a route to achieving them.

- Remember the **wealth of time**: the main purpose of money is to buy time and freedom.

- **Don't overcomplicate** your financial affairs: **consolidate** your accounts and automate as many of your behaviours as you can.

- Outsourcing your finances to **professional advisors** will save you time, make your life **easier** and help you **achieve your goals faster**.

- Goals don't ensure success, but certainly increase the likeliness of it.

- If you're struggling to think of a plan, ask yourself; What would you like to accomplish in life that will require planning, money and time?

- Lie: Money is the only type of wealth. In fact, **there are 5 types of wealth:** Financial (money), Social (relationships), Physical (health), Mental (knowledge, faith), Time (freedom). The pursuit of financial wealth can rob you of the others. Don't let that happen.

- For anyone who is employed and isn't 100% sure of their current available work benefits, I find that this is a helpful email template below to send on to your HR dept:

> *Having spoken to a financial advisor they have asked me for a few bits of information so I can ensure I'm doing everything as well as possible. Would you please help me to answer the following questions as I'm not 100% certain on each one. Thanks*
>
> ***With my pension.***
>
> *1. Can you confirm what the maximum contribution I can make which the company will match?*
>
> *2. Are my contributions set up on a salary sacrifice basis?*
>
> *3. If not, can these please be set up this way?*
>
> *4. If they can be set up on salary sacrifice, will the company add in the NI saving to the pension?*

With regards to benefits.

1. *What is the level of any death in service provided?*

2. *Do you provide any critical illness cover?*

3. *If I was to be off sick, how much would I receive as sick pay & for how long?*

4. *Is there any form of income protection available on top of this?*

Conclusion

I hope you've enjoyed this book and found it a helpful guide on your path to a wealthy life. What many people really want from money is the ability to stop thinking about it. This may sound a bit ironic when I've just spent so much time on the subject, but a wealthy life is simply one that allows us to achieve our preferred lifestyle. To have enough money, when we need it, for all purposes, both known and unknown. Then we can stop thinking about money and enjoy the moment.

We all want different things from life but, in essence, it's about making sure the money we earn from our work is available when we need it to make our lives as enjoyable as possible; that it provides this for us as long as we need it to (potentially 100 years) and creates better foundations for future generations to come.

This is achievable for all of us, when we know how. It's something that takes time, effort and planning to achieve, and it's an evolving process. As I've said throughout the book, life is split into different seasons; a fascinating series of stages that we all go through. Passing through the early years of innocence, experimenting in our adolescence, beginning our careers, perhaps starting families and putting down roots, achieving more senior positions at work, becoming grandparents, retiring and growing old gracefully. There will always be moments that change the course of a human life. These can strike at any time, and they happen to everyone. There are good times, bad times, easy times, hard times and everything in between. We are different people in each decade of our lives and understanding how things will change – including ourselves – allows us to fail from time to time in order to learn how to fail less in the future.

We face endless choices throughout our lives, and the main purpose of this book has been to emphasise the choices people face which involve the most significant financial decisions. The more we can understand these catalytic events, the more robust we are in the face of change, unexpected incidents and opportunities, which also makes those major choices easier to make, because we are then prepared for every event. It's about highlighting the major paths in life, and I have tried to cover off the topics that will help you move forward successfully at each stage. There will be people who experience some things sooner and others who go through the same things later in life, and the size of the monetary decisions we face are different for everyone. You can add or take away multiple zeros to or from a salary, house price or retirement income, but it doesn't change the fact that, whatever the amounts of money involved, you need to consider your risks, understand your thought processes and your goals and think about how your decisions will affect other people in your life.

People whose ultimate goal is just to have more money, without any clear idea of how much they need or what they will use it for, often get stuck. It's also important to be wary of becoming entrapped by spending – when, rather than using money to build a life, your life is built around money. Part of this comes from the belief that spending money will make you happier. It can do, but for many people it doesn't, either because it never will or because they haven't yet discovered the kind of spending that brings real joy. Some people decide that the reason they are not getting enough joy from their spending is that they are not spending enough, so they double down, again and again. I've often wondered how many personal bankruptcies and financial troubles were caused by spending that brought no joy to begin with. It must be a sizeable number, and it's a double loss: not only do you end up in trouble, but you didn't even have fun getting there.

I always remember how one of my first clients first taught me this lesson. He was an elderly gentleman, single and relatively wealthy. He would come into the bank I worked for at that time to assess what we could do in terms of returns on his investments compared with other banks, and I asked him why he didn't spend some more of his money. He told me he had always wanted to see tigers in India but felt he couldn't afford it because it was expensive, and so he never got around to going. We sat and discussed his options for investing his money and, out of curiosity, I went online in the meeting and found a fully guided trip to India that cost around the same amount as the forecast earnings on his investments for the coming year. He said he would think about it and we carried on with the financial planning. Six months later he came back into the office and told me how he had gone home that day and booked the trip and travelled to India and seen tigers in their natural habitat and that it was one of the best things he had ever done in his life. He said he planned to do something similar every year. This stuck with me ever after.

My philosophy has always been to try to make life easier and more enjoyable for clients. This is something that can be cultivated by design. It stands on the premise that the least effective plan for financial independence is to be passive. A person who passively waits for the world to give them something better will typically still be waiting in five, ten, twenty years from now. Passive living defies Newton's third law, which states that for every action, there is an equal and opposite reaction. Essentially, no action means no result and, in my experience, a harder life. The world won't generally gift the golden opportunity you've been waiting for; it doesn't tend to work that way. The most effective form of living is active, and this implies taking knowing steps today to set yourself up for future success. Creating a plan; a route to where you want to go. It's about strategically preparing for what may lie ahead – saving more than you spend and investing wisely: insuring against things going wrong;

developing the necessary skills for future job prospects; and being able to enjoy living. The key message is that planning puts the world on your side. If you are proactive and refresh your goals constantly, the world does a lot of the heavy lifting for you.

There is a particular analogy for this that I like and use in my own life. I imagine myself on a sailing voyage, and I know what my destination is and the general direction I want to go in. The fastest route is clearly the most direct, but I know that at times I will want to go off course when the sirens of life occasionally call me ashore. I may stop off at islands to climb mountains and swim in turquoise bays. I will want to visit must-see destinations along the way. I might learn to sail a bigger or better vessel and recruit a crew. I might need to stop for repairs from time to time just to be able to continue my journey. I know that I will reach my destination so long as I stay on course, but the journey has to be enjoyable – or what's the point? There is nothing wrong in taking the slower, scenic route sometimes, or cutting some things out at other times to get to the next location faster, always using our GPS to stay on course to the final destination.

I like the idea that wealth is a state of mind and that when someone else tells you what you should be doing with your money or your life, the best response is often, "You might be right." The next time someone disagrees with you or criticises you, just shrug your shoulders and say, "You might be right!"

and watch the energy change. Focus on what's right for you at any point in your life. Keep your own goals in mind.

There is an old joke is about two hikers who come across a grizzly bear in the woods. One starts to run, and the other yells, "You're crazy, you can't outrun a bear!" The runner replies: "I don't have to run faster than the bear. I only have to run faster than you." All success is relative to someone else – usually those immediately around you. It's important that your plan is your own. Be inspired by others and maybe let them do some life experiments on your behalf but, ultimately, your path is always your own.

It's easy to get caught on committing to an unfulfilling path. Just like checking in with a doctor, check your financial GPS once or twice a year to ensure your actions still match your goals and you're still on course to your destination. Are there roadblocks, short cuts, more scenic routes on your journey? Have your goals or priorities evolved, or have you learnt something new which improves your clarity or conviction? Are your foundations stronger or more exposed? Family changes, marriages, divorce and the deaths of those you know can change perspectives. New jobs can change everything, especially in your wealth-building stage. Technological advancements can make some things become a reality much earlier than we expected.

Let me end with a wise quote from the French writer and

philosopher, Montesquieu, written 275 years ago: "If you only wished to be happy, this could be easily accomplished; but we wish to be happier than other people, and this is always difficult, for we believe others to be happier than they are."

Money can be complicated. There's a human element that can defy logic: it's personal; it's messy; it's emotional. Now that you've read this book and have, I hope, a better perspective on your finances, I would strongly recommend you consider where you currently are and where you want to go next. I've created a short five-minute quiz for you to complete if you choose. This will give you an overall score on your general financial position and help you identify the areas to prioritise and focus on, so you maintain momentum in your journey.

Feel free to get in touch if you have any questions or want to discuss your quiz results.

Wishing you every success,

Ben Chapman

Use the QR code below to take the 5 minute quiz.

About the author

Ben Chapman, age 41, is a Chartered Financial Planner and Fellow of the Chartered Insurance Institute, who has been advising clients for over 20 years, working with every type of client, from ages 8 to 88. With prizes for the highest exam marks in the country under his belt, he runs his own financial advisory business and believes that managing finances can maximize joy in life. His curiosity and love for studying have led him to become a beacon in the industry, making lives easier through his Financial GPS.